Mark Morris

DOMESDAY
REVISITED

A traveller's guide

SEVERN HOUSE PUBLISHERS

This title first published in 1987 by
Severn House Publishers Ltd of
40–42 William IV Street, London WC2N 4DF

British Library Cataloguing in Publication Data
   Domesday revisited: a traveller's guide.
   1. Normans——Great Britain   2. Great Britain
   ——Antiquities
   I. Title
   941.02   DA195

   ISBN 0–7278–2081–8
   ISBN 0–7278–2101–6 Pbk

To Carolyn Morris

Typeset by Inforum Limited, Portsmouth.
Printed and bound by Butler & Tanner Limited,
Frome and London

CONTENTS

AUTHOR'S NOTE

I would like to thank all the many people who have been of such help with the preparation of this book; it would be invidious to single out any particular one of them.

TEXT ACKNOWLEDGEMENTS

Thanks go to Denys Baker for preparing the maps and site plans which appear throughout the book, and to the staff of the Public Record Office for their advice and assistance.

Extracts from The Battle of Maldon are taken from The Earliest English Poems translated by Michael Alexander (Penguin Classics, 1977) pp 28–29, 114–123, © Michael Alexander, 1966, 1977.

Extracts from The Anglo-Saxon Chronicle are taken from the Everyman's Classics edition, translated by G.N. Garmonsway, and published by J M Dent, 1972.

PHOTOGRAPHIC ACKNOWLEDGEMENTS

Pages 26, 38, 41, 50, 77, 119, 124: National Survey of Churches. Pages 89, 99: David Hall. Page 132: Lucy Lloyd. Page 140: Ben Kirst. All other photographs have been supplied by the author.

Preface

This book is something of a hybrid: part guide, part history, part speculation, part imagination, part description. It is a travel book, but one that is operating in two time periods; the first the modern England with its ease of transport and an interest in its past, the second the passing of the Anglo-Saxon period and the coming of the Normans, when transport was by no means easy and the interest in history was confined to a few rare literate people or to tales handed down from memory to memory and recounted around a hearth.

For those travels, I have chosen seven places in the England covered by the Domesday Book of 1086, each with its own special atmosphere, and each with something to say about the 11th century, and, also, in amongst the ancient ruins and long-standing buildings, something about the 20th. In doing so, there must be an immediate apology. The seven sites are all in southern England or the Midlands for, rather like modern Britain, Norman England was biased to the south. The Domesday record does not venture further north than Yorkshire, and even in those more northerly areas it does cover the entries are less comprehensive. Substantial Anglo-Saxon remains are rarer in the north than in the south, partly through destruction wreaked by the Normans themselves. If there is also a preponderance of churches finding their way into these pages, that partly reflects the inevitable fact that of all the types of building from the period, churches have had the best chances of survival.

I have also tried to choose sites that are less well known, while still reflecting 11th-century life, for these are less likely to be adulterated by later additions that so easily give a false picture. The sites also favour the description of the life of ordinary people rather than the royal court or the chief magnates: sites such as York or the Tower of London are already well documented and described for the visitor, and their inclusion here would have meant the exclusion of a less well-known but potentially interesting site. To reflect what the Normans found when they arrived – the end of the Anglo-Saxon society rather than the foundation of the Norman – I have avoided (with one or two exceptions) any buildings that were completed after 1086. That, of course, includes the programme of cathedral building which the Normans started, but unfortunately that programme was so thorough that not a single Anglo-Saxon cathedral survives.

Anglo-Norman society, particularly its agriculture but sometimes also its landscape, seems far away now. But it is always worth recalling that a farmer of the time would still find something to recognise in, say, Spain, where the residue of feudal farming can still be seen, and if no one now pays rent for their strips of land in kind, places can still be found where rents for ground-plots of houses are handed over in hens. Yet in that Anglo-Norman society can be found the basis of our systems of law and many of our institutions, as well as the plans of many of our towns and villages.

1

That alone rewards a travel of the imagination through their lands, quite apart from the sheer fascination and beauty of much that they physically left behind.

*   *   *

Throughout the book I have used Church with a capital C to refer to the ecclesiastical body, and church with a small c to refer to actual buildings. Similarly, I have used the word Scandinavian to include Denmark as well as Norway and Sweden.

The monetary values of the 11th century are not really convertible into modern currency – if you grow much, if not all, of your produce the whole concept of money and what you use it for takes on a different perspective. As a rough guide, the legal price of an ox in the early 11th century was 30d, that of a sheep 4d, and a slave usually cost £1. Land values are much more difficult to quantify: a shilling probably would have bought an acre in the 10th century. Thus someone with an income of £8 to £10 a year was well-off; but in contrast the very rich were very rich indeed and individual items of jewellery could be worth £15 or more. Quite a number of monetary units were used, but the most common was the system of pounds, shillings and pence in use in Britain until 1971: 12 pence (d) = 1 shilling (s) and 20 shillings (or 240d) = 1 pound (£).

A Domesday Introduction

While a Norman archer was loosing an arrow into Harold's eye on the battlefield at Hastings on that fateful day in 1066, someone was leaning over a large table in China sorting out small pieces of movable type for a printing press. A clock, driven by water, would soon tell the time in Peking; gunpowder was being manufactured; Ts'ui Po was painting his delicate masterpieces; and Seishonagon was writing *The Pillow Book*. In Burma and India great temples were encrusted with decoration and sculpture, or sought to portray in architecture the dwellings of the gods, while in Central America enormous irrigation schemes requiring an advanced level of engineering skills were being constructed. In the eyes of modern Western culture gunpowder was more than a century away, and printing was the invention of Gutenberg. If any contemporary had had the chance to travel the world in the 11th century, north-western Europe would have seemed no more than a developing area compared with the civilisation of China; the Norman horses would have baulked at the first sound of gunfire; and Western art, if intricate and detailed, would have seemed crude and unnatural.

When looking back to the achievements of Anglo-Saxon and Norman England such global comparisons lurk in the recesses of the memory to remind us of the incomparability of civilisations. 1066 has become a seminal date, the point at which Britain's history is so often thought of (however erroneously) as beginning; not for nothing do aristocratic pedigrees hope to trace their ancestry to the Normans, in much the same way that Americans gain extra prestige if their families go back to the Revolution. But just as there was an America before 1776, albeit an embryonic entity, so there was an England before 1066, an embryonic country. In a sense 1066 *is* seminal, for it marks a point from which the cohesive history of Britain can continuously be traced until Britain actually ruled and controlled Burmese temples and Indian mountains. It is also the last point of history in which Britain was successfully invaded by another country.

England was, in 1066, a cultured and advanced society, at least in European terms, and it swallowed up, merged with, and dictated the development of the Normans who crossed the Channel as much as it was altered and dictated to by them. The bare facts of the Norman Conquest would seem somewhat fantastic, were they not true. A force of perhaps 8000 men crossed the Channel and conquered a country with a population of between $1\frac{1}{2}$ and 2 million, partly through one single devastating battle. The whole picture was, of course, more complex, and to understand this it is worth retracing the history that led up to the invasion.

The Departure of the Romans and the Saxon invasions: 410–600

The story starts as far back as the withdrawal of the Romans from the island (usually dated to AD 410). Some time before this departure the eastern seaboard of

Britain had been harried by raids and attacks from across the North Sea, and, as was common Roman practice, some of these pirates may have been invited to settle alongside the indigenous Celto-British and themselves guard the coast against further incursions. After the legions had left, the province split into smaller kingdoms, and one of their kings, Vortigern, invited more Saxons to fight for him and gave them land in the east. On hearing this, further settlers followed across the North Sea. Sometime during the second half of the 5th century these Saxon immigrants – Angles, Saxons, Frisians, and Jutes, from the shores of modern Germany, Denmark, Holland and Belgium – revolted against the indigenous British, but were decisively defeated at the battle of Mons Badonicus, an unidentified site that may have been Badbury Rings in Dorset, and an era of relative calm lasted until the middle of the 6th century.

Between 550 and 600, the Saxons gradually pushed the British back to the west, taking over most of southern England, the Midlands, and northern England, in a series of fits and starts which saw dominance fluctuate between the two different races, although the Saxons never entirely subjugated Wessex (central southern England), and their immigrant settlements were mostly confined to the eastern half of the country. The subsequent internal merger of the two different peoples left only the kingdoms of Dumnonia (Devon and Cornwall), Strathclyde, and Wales as Celtic-speaking areas and the forerunner of modern Welsh, Gallic, and old Cornish. The first stage of the North Sea immigration was essentially over.

Northumbria, Mercia and Wessex: 600–790

The period from 600 to 790 saw the conversion of most of England to Christianity, the rise of monasticism (it was the age of Bede), the dominance of two great kingdoms, Northumbria and Mercia, and the emergence of another, Wessex. Under King Edwin (616–632), Northumbria became a unified and Christian area, his influence extending from Scotland to south of the Humber and into Wales, and Bede saw his reign as one of peace and plenty. The area remained an entity after his death, in spite of regular warfare with the other kingdoms and the occasional collapse of Northumbrian royal control, and the boundary between Northumbria and Mercia, a westward extension of the Humber estuary, was the major political division in England.

The kingdom of Mercia came to prominence at the end of the 7th century, thanks to the expansionist activities of a heathen king, Penda, and under Aethelbald (716–757) it controlled, directly or indirectly, most of England south of the Humber[1]. His successor, King Offa (757–796), was one of the outstanding political

1. We shall meet Aethelbald in the chapter on Brixworth.

4

figures between the departure of the Romans and the coming of the Normans. He extinguished some of the smaller kingdoms (Kent, Sussex, and Lindsey), controlled East Anglia, instituted currency reforms, encouraged the growth of commercial activity between England and the Continent, and built the dyke between Mercia and Wales that still carries his name.

Wessex, home to the West Saxons, slowly extended its influence from central southern England to the west country during the 7th century, attempted the same ends to the east, and even during the period of Mercian domination during the 8th century succeeded in maintaining a royal dynasty that would lead to Alfred the Great.

The Viking Invasions: 793–871

In 793 came the first signs that the history of England was to undergo a profound change. The monastery at Lindisfarne was sacked by new raiders from across the North Sea and in the next two years, Jarrow and Iona suffered the same fate. The nature of the disaster to contemporary eyes was not just that the east coast was seeing bloodshed and destruction – those were common enough events throughout Britain – but that holy Christian places were being destroyed by heathens. These raiders were Vikings: the tenor of North Sea expansion had shifted from the Saxon areas of the 6th century further north, to Denmark, Norway, and Sweden.

Initially their expeditions were nothing more than pirate raids to remove riches and captives, and in the meantime the power of Mercia was shaken first by defeat at the hands of the East Angles in the 820s, and then by the mercurial rise of Wessex under King Egbert (802–839). For a period he controlled England up to the Humber, until Mercia restored some sort of equilibrium between the two countries. The stage was set for a classic struggle for dominance between them, but a completely different threat intervened: what had been Viking raiding parties became serious incursions and then invasions. The Vikings attacked East Anglia in 841, Northumbria in 844, and in 855 wintered for the first time in England (on the Isle of Sheppey). But Mercia and Wessex did not realise the significance of these events until 865, when a Danish army landed in East Anglia, one so large and formidable that the East Angles instantly came to terms and supplied them with horses. From this base the raiders attacked Northumbria, took York, and invaded Mercia, who, in spite of Wessex help, had to make peace. By 874 the Vikings were masters of Northumbria, the eastern regions of England, and had placed a vassal king on the throne of Mercia. Behind their shifting battlefronts came settlers, moving across the North Sea to East Anglia and the north-east with their customs and their language, and, by rounding Scotland, they moved into Ireland, the Outer Isles, Cumbria, and the Isle of Man. Only the mountainous regions of Scotland and Wales, and the kingdom of Wessex where they had been repulsed at the battle of Ashdown in 871, were free of their presence.

Alfred the Great: 871–899

Alfred became King of Wessex at the age of 23, and by 875 was the last adult survivor of the old English royal houses. By then the Viking army had divided into two, one half moving into Northumbria and even into southern Scotland, the other continuing to attack Wessex from its East Anglian bases. By 878 Alfred was forced to withdraw into the Somerset marshes, but called together his forces and decisively defeated the Danish army at Edington. The Danish leader, Guthrum, was forced into Christianity, and the Danes eventually left Wessex for East Anglia. Skirmishes continued between the two areas, but in 886 southern England was more formally divided up by treaty. The frontier ran along the mouth of the Thames and then followed the River Lea, continued to Bedford, along the Ouse to Watling Street and then along the old Roman road: in effect, a line running from the mouth of the Thames west-north-west to Shrewsbury. The South Welsh and the West Mercians submitted to the overlordship of Alfred, while Gwynedd in North Wales joined the Danes. While these two opposing groups faced each other across the boundaries of Watling Street and the mountains of mid-Wales, an army of Danes who had gone to fight in Gaul returned to attack Kent and Essex in 892. The Northumbrian and East Anglian Danes attacked West Mercia in concert with this southern army, but could not defeat Alfred's forces. The Northumbrians came to some sort of accommodation with Wessex, and the King of Gwynedd submitted to Alfred.

Edward, Aethelstan, and Edgar: 899–978

If Alfred succeeded in establishing a military equilibrium with the Danes, his successor Edward (899–924) went on the offensive. He collaborated with his sister Aethelflaed, Queen of Mercia, and, by the skilful use of forts as strategic bases, they conquered the Danish heartlands of the central Midlands and East Anglia. With the death of his sister and the submission of Wales, Edward was master of all south of the Humber by 919, and by the end of his reign he had secured the submission of Northumbria, which had its own problems of west coast incursions by the Irish Vikings, and of York. His son, Aethelstan (924–939) then conquered York and Northumbria (as opposed to leaving them as vassal kingdoms), and actually threatened the Scots, who promptly formed a coalition with the Irish Danes and elements from the Isles, only to be defeated. Aethelstan ruled as undisputed master of England, and for the first time the country became an independent political unit.

It did not last for, in a confused and swiftly changing period from 939 to 955, the

Scandinavians regained control of Northumbria, York, and the East Midlands. Edgar (959–978) restored the supremacy of Wessex, and was the titular head of England as a whole, but the acquiescence of Northumbria, East Anglia, York and Mercia seems to have been a matter of expediency rather than through any overwhelming military or political superiority on the part of Edgar.

Aethelred the Unready: 978–1016

Edgar's son Edward was murdered shortly after the death of his father, and his half-brother Aethelred (978–1016), known rather unfairly to later generations as the Unready, became king. His problems were two-fold: first, the almost independent power of the earldoms of the areas outside Wessex itself, and second, a renewed wave of Scandinavian attacks across the North Sea. The Vikings had discovered a new and highly successful tactic: after ravaging an area (and they were never decisively engaged in Aethelred's reign) they were prepared to be bought off for what amounted to staggering sums – £10,000 in 991, rising to £48,000 in 1012. By 1010 East Anglia had again fallen to the Danes, and 1013 saw a more serious invasion led by the King of Denmark, Swein. He landed in the Humber, and the Danelaw, those old Danish areas in Alfred's division, immediately submitted to him without a fight. Oxford, Winchester and Bath quickly followed suit when they saw his destruction of the countryside as the Danish army crossed Watling Street. London held out for a while, but then surrendered, and Aethelred fled to Normandy.

Aethelred's relations with Normandy proved important in the light of later events. In 991 the Pope had had to mediate between him and Richard, Duke of Normandy, as the Normans were of Scandinavian origin, and the Vikings had been using the Dukedom as a continental base for their attacks on England. Both agreed not to harbour each other's enemies, and in 1002 Aethelred married Richard's daughter, thus introducing Norman blood into the English royal household. His stay in Normandy was not a long one, though, for in 1014 Swein died. His son Cnut became king in the Danelaw, but Wessex asked Aethelred to return, in spite of their reservations about his harsh and sometimes unjust style of kingship. Cnut attacked Wessex, and on Aethelred's death in 1016 his son Edmund (called Ironside) attempted to organise resistance[2]. But he too died in the same year, and the Dane Cnut became king over Wessex as well as the Danelaw.

Cnut, Harold I, and Harthacnut: 1016–1042

In the space of 30 years England had swung dramatically from being an independent, self-contained kingdom to being an element of a North Sea empire, for

2. As will be seen in the chapter on Deerhurst.

Cnut was king of Denmark and Norway as well as England. He also seems to have been a secure and successful monarch: Scandinavians and English both held high office, he confirmed and extended traditional customs and laws in his Code of 1020–21, he married Aethelred's Norman widow Emma, and his position was such that he could spend periods away from England in Denmark and, indeed, travelled to Rome. His death in 1035 produced a complicated situation: his son, Harthacnut, was more concerned with problems in the Scandinavian sections of the empire, and Harold, Cnut's son by his first marriage, became King of England. Two members of English royal blood, Aethelred's sons Alfred and Edward, returned from Normandy, probably to stake their claims to the throne. Alfred was mutilated and died and Edward fled back to Normandy. Harold died in 1040, and Harthacnut returned to unite Denmark and England again, but he himself died two years later. At this point the Kings of Denmark and Norway both had ambitions for the English throne, but, in fact, Edward, known to us as the Confessor, was invited back from Normandy to continue the ancient dynasty of the English royal family.

Edward the Confessor: 1042–1066

Edward's situation was paradoxical. Although of English royal blood, he had spent much of his life in Normandy, with its synthesis of Scandinavian and Frankish cultures. In England he inherited a number of magnates who had been appointed in the reign of Cnut and who held considerable personal power in their own regions, those ancient areas that were based on former kingdoms – Leofric in Mercia, Siward in Northumberland, and Godwine, Earl of Wessex. The immediate threat was that of invasion by Magnus of Norway, which was pre-empted first by naval action and then by the death of Magnus in 1047.

In 1051 the struggles between king and earls came to a head. Godwine, with his sons, (themselves in positions of regional power) defied the king over what looks in retrospect to have been a pretext. Leofric and Siward supported the king, civil war was only just avoided, the Godwines fled to Flanders and to Ireland, and Edward banished his wife Edith, Godwine's daughter, to a nunnery. In 1052 the Godwines returned with a large force but Leofric and Siward preferred accommodation to warfare, and persuaded the king to accept them back. As part of the agreement some of the Normans – bishops and soldiers – that Edward had introduced to the country were forced to return to Normandy. From then on the power of the Godwine family grew, though it suffered a check when the Northumbrians forced one of Godwine's sons, Tostig, out of the earldom because of his oppressive rule. Nonetheless, by the 1060s, another son, Harold, was the most powerful man in the country after the king.

Edward's marriage was childless. The details of the question of his successor, so crucial to later events, have remained shrouded in obscurity, and the interpretation of events rather depended on whose side one took, the Normans or the English. A potential candidate was Edward, son of Edmund Ironside and thus of royal blood, and in 1057 he returned from exile in Hungary, probably with Edward's agreement, and certainly with the support of Harold Godwineson, but he immediately died. Edward may also have promised the crown to Normandy – the Normans certainly claimed so, and fixed their history books to reinforce the point. They also claimed that Harold, on a royal mission to Normandy, had sworn to uphold William's claim to the throne; the English charged that the oath was administered by trickery, with William hiding holy relics under the tablecloth to turn what was probably an expedient reply into a binding oath. Whatever promises had or had not been made, when Edward died in January 1066, Harold, brother-in-law to the dead king, and the man with the most military and political experience in England, seemed the obvious choice and he was immediately crowned. Those on the opposite shores of the Channel and the North Sea had been watching like vultures around a dying body, and instantly swung into action. The Normans mobilised, to use a modern expression, and so did Harald Hardrada, King of Norway, with the help of Harold's exiled brother Tostig. Even the King of Denmark contemplated the invasion of England, and the appearance of Halley's comet in April only seemed to confirm the multiple threat that lay over the new king and his kingdom.

The Norman Invasion: 1066

The immediate danger seemed to come from the Normans, and Harold called out his army, composed of a general levy called the *fyrd* but with a core of seasoned troops of Danish origin, the *housecarles* or royal bodyguards. He stationed this army on the Channel while William of Normandy built and gathered an invasion fleet. In fact, Tostig landed first in a rather hopeless attempt at invasion; after being driven off the southern shores, his force was destroyed in Lincolnshire. The Normans were delayed by consistently contrary winds, and Harold was forced to stand down the levies on September 8th, as they desperately needed to return to the land to catch up with their farming. Almost immediately the expected attack came, but it was in a totally different quarter: Harald Hardrada with the ubiquitous Tostig at his side landed at the Humber and moved on York. Northumbrian and Mercian forces moved to oppose him, but were cut to pieces at the battle of Fulford with the loss of many valuable fighting men. Harold swiftly moved his army north, gathering the *fyrd* as he went, and, after a famous and remarkable forced march, surprised the Vikings at the battle of Stamford Bridge on September 25th. Hardrada and Tostig were killed, and the Viking force decimated. Over 200 longships had sailed up the Ouse but only 24 sailed away.

On September 27th, while Harold's forces were still clearing up after the battle, the wind in the Channel changed and the Norman force set sail. It landed unopposed at Pevensey, and swiftly moved to Hastings where it hastily built a small wooden castle. London was wide open, but at this stage William did not dare to leave his beachhead exposed, and Harold hurried south[3]. He left London on October 12th, rendezvoused with his various forces at an apple tree on the 13th (a Friday), and moved into position seven miles from the Norman camp that night. There, at first light the next morning, his forces drew up on a good defensive situation on Senlac ridge, fronted by a slope. William, on hearing that Harold had occupied the ridge, moved his army up to meet him. The battle started around 9.30 that morning, and lasted all day. William's principal military advantages – his well-armoured cavalry knights, who had no equivalent in the English forces, and his superiority in numbers of archers – were nullified by the English position, the former because they could not charge up a slope effectively, and the latter because, ironically, they relied on the opposing archers to supply them with arrows, and the lack of return fire meant that they were short of ammunition. The forces were therefore well matched, and the critical moment came only when William could use the superiority of his cavalry.

An attack by Breton forces fighting with the Norman army up the slope to the English right flank was repulsed, and the levies, previously held in check, could not resist chasing down the slope after them. William swung his cavalry to intercept and slaughter the charging English, and later in the battle seems to have copied the tactic on the other flank. But the remaining English held firm on the ridge, and late in the afternoon William risked a final all-out assault. The Normans gained the top of the slope, and the fiercest and bloodiest hand-to-hand fighting of the day took place. While it was at its height Harold was hit in the eye by an arrow, and then cut down by four charging Norman knights who had seen him fall. The English fought on, but the battle was lost, and as night fell and the remnants of the English army made what escape they could, the Normans were masters of the field.

The core of the experienced English fighting troops and their leaders were killed at the battles of Fulford and Hastings. In addition, there was no obvious candidate around whom English resistance to the Normans could congregate. The earls of Northumbria and Mercia, Morcar and Edwin, did not command the respect required, and had anyway been defeated at Fulford. The sole survivor of the English royal line, Edgar the Aetheling, was still only 15, and although a coalition of Mercia, Northumbria, London and the Archbishops contemplated crowning him, they decided the risks were too great. William did not advance on London immediately; instead he moved along the south coast, destroying as he went, approached London, and then circled through Surrey, Hampshire and Berkshire. The effects of his

3. He may have heard the news of William's landing while actually marching south.

destruction were so great that they can be traced in the Domesday Book entries twenty years later. Winchester was surrendered by Queen Edith, and London gave in. William was crowned in Westminster Abbey on Christmas Day: the duke had become a king.

Norman Consolidation: 1067–1087

As soon as he was crowned, William started a programme of castle building, moved more troops over from Normandy, and allocated areas to some of his leading supporters, who included a smattering of Franks, Bretons, and other nationalities as well as Normans. The surviving major English figures were kept at court and taken to Normandy when William returned across the Channel in February 1067. English revolt started to ferment, but it was sporadic, uncoordinated and doomed to failure. Nonetheless, William had to return to England in December to deal with it. Opposition was crushed in the southwest, Mercia and Northumberland, and castles built at Exeter, Nottingham and York to control the dissident areas, but in 1069 the Danes struck along the east coast, anchored off the Humber, and Yorkshire rose up. The forces joined, and with Edgar the Aetheling among their number, took York. But when William moved north, the alliance fell apart: Edgar returned to Scotland, and the Danes eventually accepted a profitable retreat with their booty. William then decided on a course of savage destruction, the 'Harrying of the North' as it has become known, in which the whole area, including northern Mercia, was completely laid waste by Norman forces split into small groups. Nothing that could be useful, such as animals, houses, farming equipment, and no one who fell into the hands of the Normans, was spared. The action not only destroyed all resistance, it destroyed the countryside, so that often little remained for the compilers of Domesday to record. English resistance continued in the fen country (led by Hereward the Wake), but that last remnant of English pride had been extinguished by 1071.

William then strengthened the troublesome border with Wales, and in 1072 attacked Scotland in a combined operation by land and sea which led to the Scottish king accepting him as overlord. Unrest now came from his own followers, and revolts that emanated in Hereford and Northumbria had to be put down. However, for the rest of his reign, William's major problems were in Normandy, and England was secure enough, apart from a Danish threat in 1085[4], for William to take troops from England to Normandy. There he successfully dealt with revolt from within Normandy, devastating Maine in the process, and conducted intermittent warfare with the King of France, who had not been pleased to find that an ostensibly vassal duke had also become a king. In the middle of the latter confrontation William fell ill and died

4. The fears of a Danish invasion in 1085 are described in the chapter on Colchester.

on September 9th 1087. His end was an anti-climax – his servants despoiled his body, the funeral had to be hurried as the corpse soon began to smell, and part of Caen caught fire as the cortège processed through – but the Norman dynasty in England had been founded.

The Domesday Survey

The Norman Conquest can be seen as the culmination of a wider process during which England had been subject to attack, invasion, and settlement by Scandinavians. With the Norman invasion the direction merely shifted from the North Sea to the Channel, and after the first interlacing of English and Norman affairs and royal lines such a change of axis may have been inevitable. In origin the Normans were themselves Vikings, and their extraordinary explosion into the affairs of Europe in the 11th century – they were also spectacularly active in the Mediterranean as a whole, and in Sicily and southern Italy in particular – might be described as a renewal of those restless, expansive Viking energies, honed and developed by their experiences as a settled unit, within the wider horizons of Frankish history and culture. The objectives were now more direct, and were combined with a military discipline and technique – castle building and cavalry – that was for the moment unmatched in their quarter of the world.

At the same time, they seem to have been something of an unimaginative people. They were manipulators, not innovators: even their castle designs probably owe much to Middle Eastern models, and their churches and cathedrals to Mediterranean examples. The Norman conquest of England had one major difference from Scandinavian invasions: no mass immigration of settlers followed the military. Normans certainly came over, but the change in England was one of the ruling class, not of new influxes to the mass of the ordinary working population. The constant warfare that seems to permeate the whole history of the period must also be kept in perspective. While destruction could be widespread, and the initial barbarity of the Normans and their heavy taxation was hated, the peasant farmer was probably far more frightened of famine or blight than bloodshed, and more likely to suffer both than a violent end. Other masters had come and gone; from the perspective of farming history the Normans were a new name in a long list.

It was the style of the Normans, partly because they were only a ruling class, and partly because of their lack of innovative imagination, to confirm the structures and laws of areas they conquered and adapt them to their own ends rather than impose a totally new system of law and custom. Although many records have been lost, it is becoming increasingly clear that in England the Normans were very fortunate. Here they found an extremely efficient and advanced administrative system, used to keeping records in writing, itself an indication that, in spite of the military and political turmoils of preceding reigns, the bulk of activity was sufficiently undisturbed for such an infrastructure to evolve. William adapted this infrastructure to his own ends, in particular to reinforce the feudal system that allowed the Normans the discipline for their energies. One major result of the synthesis was the remarkable survey known to us as the Domesday Book.

The Domesday Book: 1086

The plans for the compilation of the Domesday Book were drawn up at the royal Christmas Council of 1085, and seem to have been put into effect immediately. There has been much debate on the original aims of the survey. The Danish threats of 1085 and the need to call up a large army may have brought home to William how little he knew of the country and its capacity to provide a fighting force. In addition, much of the land was apportioned to the Norman lords as landholders, taking over the estates of their Anglo-Saxon equivalents, although the actual owner of all the land in the kingdom was the king himself, as it had been under the Anglo-Saxons. The king retained large areas under his direct control as royal estates, and so did the Church, acting as tenants-in-chief to the king. The lords themselves regularly sub-let to other tenants, and in the wholesale change to Norman landholders there must have been much confusion and dispute, not to mention a straightforward lack of detailed knowledge of the extent and wealth of all these lands. The Domesday survey was designed to supply that knowledge: with it the extent of feudal military obligations could be assessed, it could provide the basis for taxation and the suppression of tax-avoidance, and disputes over landholdings could be sorted out.

The survey was based on the standard English unit of the shire (county), although it went no further north than Yorkshire on one side and the Lake District on the other, so tenuous was the Norman hold on the old kingdom of Northumbria. The shires were divided into areas known generally as hundreds, and in the first stage of the process of compilation, representatives of each village as well as the major landholders went to the Hundred Courts to provide information on the areas in which they lived and to swear to its validity. In most cases they were probably confirming written records that had already been lodged with the court, and the survey could not have been conducted without this basic system of administration and the extent and efficiency of written records that the Normans inherited from the Anglo-Saxons.

The elementary unit of the survey was the manor, whose exact composition varied considerably around the country, but can be thought of as the equivalent to a rural estate. This was a more practical base unit than the village itself as villages could be divided between more than one manor, and some manors might have land in more than one village. The first information to which the representatives had to swear concerned the land itself: the name of the manor, how much land it held and who held it, how many plough teams were owned by the manor farm and how many by men living on the manor, the extent of woodland, meadow and pasture, the number of mills, fisheries and other relevant details such as vineyards. They then had to supply the numbers of people (normally men and heads of households) who were living on the manor, and their status: freemen, men with various grades of obligation and service, or slaves. They also had to supply information on the numbers and kinds of livestock. Finally they had to supply the value of the whole manor.

Ideally the Hundred Court had to prepare this information for three different dates: the time of Edward the Confessor (in other words, 1066, for the Normans did not recognise that Harold had ever ruled, and the Domesday Book slips up only once in referring to him as king), the date on which William gave out the land, and the present day. In practise this was not always possible, but it gave some indication of the financial performance and potential of the manor concerned – a typical entry might read 'Value then (i.e. 1066) 60s, now 90s', and sometimes carry the laconic comment 'room for 5 more ploughs'. Towns were treated in much the same way, and when this information had been gathered in the Hundred Courts, it went to the Shire Courts, and there was inspected by the royal commissioners. The country had been divided into seven (perhaps nine) circuits each consisting of a number of shires, and each the responsibility of one group of probably three commissioners – men of high rank (including bishops and abbots) who had no direct financial interest in the area they were inspecting. They checked and gathered the material, and at the same time settled disputes, although they referred the thornier cases to the king, and armed with their new knowledge probably made sure that the very high taxation of the previous year had been paid in full.

All that material went back to Winchester, and there it was condensed (with much use of abbreviations), and, as far as was possible, standardised. The entries were divided into shires, and the information then filed, not as one might expect by hundreds but under the headings of the individual major landholders, grouping all the holdings of each landholder in that county together. The Domesday Book was thus a feudal record, and one can still quickly look up who the chief landholders were and what they held. At the same time, some of the mass of detail that had come from the shires was expunged, particularly the details of the livestock. Quite clearly there was one guiding hand that supervised the sorting out of the material and the style of the entries; alas, we have no certain idea who he was.

In fact, this process does not seem to have been completed. Most of the shires were entered into one great tome now known as Volume I. But three shires –

Norfolk, Suffolk, and Essex – never reached this final form, and their records survive in what is known as Volume II. It does include a mass of information that was normally deleted, and is almost certainly a final draft awaiting reduction. It may be that the death of William stopped any further work on it; but it may also be that the eastern areas, a mixture of English and Scandinavian holdings, customs, and even language, were so complex as to be virtually impossible to rework into the standard format – how the scribes at Winchester must have blanched when they started to pour over the material that had come in from Essex[5]. The whole of the survey was done at great speed, and the initial findings may have been ready for the meeting of all major landholders that William called at Salisbury in August 1086 to swear an oath of loyalty to him; if so, he may also have required them to confirm on oath the validity of the contents of the drafts so that they could not later dispute the entries. There was certainly no appeal against the entries, and because of its rigid finality the record was much resented by the ordinary populace. It therefore became known as the Domesday Book (the Day of Judgement also allowed no appeal), although it was officially known as the Book of Winchester.

The entries were written on parchment, each folio (parchment page) measuring about $14\frac{1}{2}$ ins by $9\frac{3}{4}$ ins in the Great Domesday Book (Volume I) and about 10 ins by $7\frac{1}{2}$ ins in the Little Domesday Book (Volume II). The language is Latin, though considerably abbreviated, and the script concise and uniform, with headings and underlinings in red ink. The folios were originally bundled together in quires, nominally one to each county, but they were soon bound together into the two volumes, by the beginning of the 13th century at the very latest. Volume I is nearly 400 folios long, written on both sides with 44 lines to each side; Volume II, although it covers only three counties, includes much more material for each entry, and is over 450 folios long. Over the years both volumes have been regularly rebound, and are now the most valued possessions of the Public Records Office in London.

Such documents have been invaluable for historians, but Domesday is essentially a record, a giant filing system of statistics, something to be consulted rather than read as one might read a literary work. It can sometimes be a frustrating source: in the attempt to impose uniformity on the entries, the differences in custom and farming practice in various areas are not always clear, there are often omissions, notably towns (space was left for entries on London and Winchester, but never filled) but also, for example, the extent of pasture in Suffolk, and errors inevitably crept in. Some of these omissions derived, no doubt, from differences in interpretation by the various areas of the information required, others because of lack of time, and others still that were quite intentional in that they were outside the aegis of the survey. Castles, monks and nuns fit into this last category – all three were outside the normal

5. Other preliminary documents have also survived.

system of income and revenue, and the former were mostly under the direct control of the king. Similarly, churches rarely appear as such: the Domesday survey is interested in the manors that the richer churches or churchmen held, not in ecclesiastical buildings.

Another problem the compilers must have had was that of language. Three languages were directly involved – the Anglo-Saxon English ('Old English') that the mass of the population spoke, the Norman-French of the invaders, and the medieval Latin of the scribes and the entries. In fact, the problem was not as acute as it might appear. Latin was a *lingua franca*, and medieval Latin and the English clerics and scribes who wrote in it were well used to producing pseudo-Latin words to describe any particular agricultural practice, and this is the language used in the Domesday Book. The gulf between Anglo-Saxon and Norman-French was greater (although some Norse words had come down to the Normans): William the Conqueror himself tried to learn English but gave up, but some English noblemen could undoubtedly speak French, and many of William's compatriots clearly did not have such linguistic difficulties – intermarriages seem to have started soon after the Conquest. What gave the compilers of the Domesday Book much more trouble were the dialectal differences in various regions, where local words were (and, of course, still are) used to describe concepts or measurements that may have been exactly the same, but on the other hand may have been only broadly similar. This occurred particularly in those areas that used to be in the Danelaw, where many agricultural expressions were of recent Scandinavian origin. One example is that of the *Hundred*: to the clerks it would have been officially an administrative unit (Latin *hundredum*) into which shires were divided; but their sizes varied dramatically, and in northern counties the division was into *wapentakes*, which although broadly similar in concept may not have been exactly the same. Similarly, to the scribes the *hide* (Latin *hida*) was a unit of land measurement that was 120 acres; but the actual size of a hide, and, more to the point, the actual area of land conjured up in a man's mind when the word 'hide' was mentioned, seems to have differed widely from area to area, if the general concept was much the same. It is these differences and variations that the Domesday Book mostly skates over by attempting to impose a uniform pattern to the entries. As such, the lack of detailed definition can be infuriating for the local historian, but it must be remembered that at the time there was almost certainly no one who could define the differences in regional practices and usage, and the very process of collecting and collating the information in general was remarkable enough.

Nevertheless, if you read between the abbreviations and the bare statistics, look beyond the hand of the scribe at his bench in Winchester, copying out details in his neat and concise script, a picture of the 11th-century world begins to emerge. It is a world poised between the inheritance of the previous era and the new direction the country was to take; yet through it all the strongest impression is left by a sense of continuity, the struggle of medieval man to grow enough food to feed himself and his children and to understand something of the world around him. In that struggle the replacement of Anglo-Saxon masters by Norman lords merely changed the tone, and not the substance.

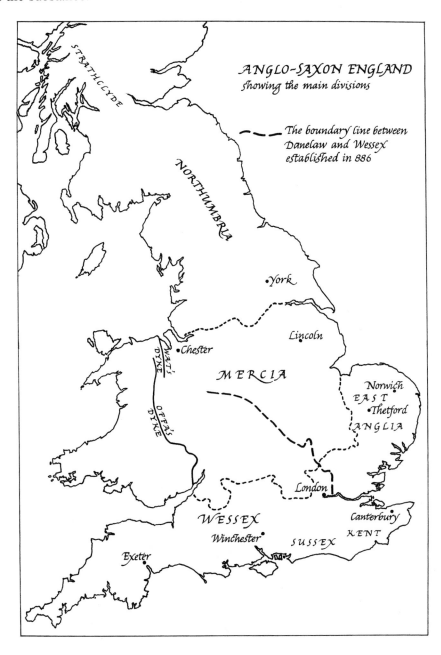

Traveller's Guide

Location of the Battle of Hastings site

TQ 746163 (metric map 199; 1-inch map 184). From Tunbridge Wells (22 miles) A21 south, then A2100. From Eastbourne (16 miles) A259 east, then B2095. From Hastings (7 miles) A2100.

The Battle site is in the care of the Department of the Environment, and includes the ruins of the Abbey built on the site by King William and consecrated in 1094. The site is open to the public, and there is a small museum, although parts of the Abbey buildings are now a private school.

Other local Norman sites

Hastings TQ 824094: Ruins of castle dating from c1070.
Pevensey TQ 645048: The landing point for the Norman army, but now landlocked. Walls of Roman fort and ruins of castle, including keep of c1100.

KILPECK

A Domesday Border

*Wills. F. Normanni ten CHIPEETE. Cadiand tenuit
T.R.E. In dnio sunt.III.car. II.ferui IIII.bouarii. . . .*

William son of Norman holds KILPECK.
Cadiand held it in the reign of King Edward. In
the lord's holdings are 3 ploughs; 2 slaves; 4
ploughmen; and 57 men with 19 ploughs. They
pay 15 sesters of honey and 10s; they neither pay
any other tax nor do service, except in the army.
Value £4.

West of the River Wye sits a grey elongated slab of mountain, sinister and brooding:
the smooth and steep-sided slopes of the ridge that mark where Wales ends and
Herefordshire begins. There, at the end of 1066, the men of the Welsh kingdom of
Ewyas guarded their border and gazed over England. Far to the right gleamed the
waters of the Bristol Channel, the raiding route for Viking ships; over to the left the
sun caught the walls of the English town of Hereford. Down in front, across a swathe
of no man's land, building-work was going on up and down the border; mounds
being thrown up, palisades being hewn and cut. The Normans, new invaders but not
unknown enemies, were moving in and fortifying the border.

The Welshmen, always eager to extend their influence beyond the stronghold of
that mountain ridge, knew this ground well. In 1049 36 ships crewed by Vikings from
Ireland – the classic oared-longships with their single squared sails – had sailed up
the Usk, and had joined forces with the Welsh under their king, Gryffydd. Together
they had poured down the ridge border, defeated the English forces under Bishop
Ealdred, and ravaged the area before returning to their mountain strongholds with
their booty and their captives. In 1055 they had allied themselves with more Irish
Vikings, this time led by an Englishman with a grievance, Aelfgar, the exiled son of
Leofric, the Earl of Mercia. In this attack they encountered a Norman for the first
time on the battlefield, for Edward the Confessor, trying to strengthen the troublesome region, had appointed his Norman nephew, Ralph, to the command of the
earldom of Hereford. The Welsh were probably not impressed with Norman
military prowess, for they routed Ralph's forces, swept into Hereford, sacked

everything inside and outside the walls, and burnt the cathedral to the ground.

Edward responded swiftly. He called out the general *fyrd* (a call to arms of all those who owed military service in the kingdom) and appointed Harold Godwineson, the future king, to lead them. Harold pushed Aelfgar and the Welsh back beyond that brooding ridge into the Black Mountains; both sides came to terms, and Aelfgar's grievances must have been substantial for he was restored to his rank and his possessions. The Vikings sailed back to Ireland with what they had gained, and the Welsh waited, until Harold led a punitive raid into Wales and dealt with the troublesome Gryffydd.

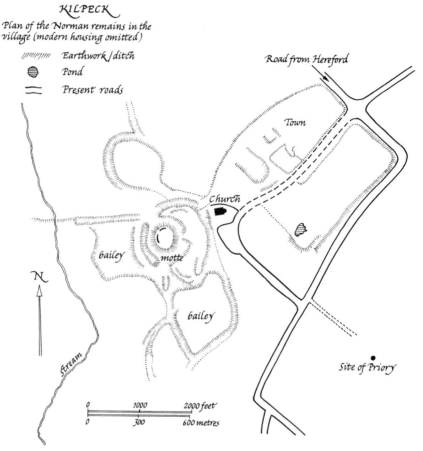

KILPECK

Plan of the Norman remains in the village (modern housing omitted)

///////// Earthwork / ditch
⊜ Pond
= Present roads

Road from Hereford

Town

Church

bailey   motte

N

bailey

Site of Priory

stream

0   1000   2000 feet
0   300   600 metres

In the meantime, Hereford was rebuilt and its defences restored. More worrying for the Welsh, however, was the fact that in the late 1040s Edward had invited Normans into the region to use their skills to build the first castles seen in Britain since the departure of the Romans. England had known fortified towns (one such site, Wareham, will be discussed later), but the art of castle-building was a new concept brought across the Channel. The swift raid would no longer mean attacking extended town walls or rampaging through valleys; instead the Welsh would come up against strongpoints, well defended and able to hold off any attack until a counter-attack could be mounted or reinforcements arrive. One of these pre-Conquest castles, Ewyas Harold, is still to be seen as a great tree-topped mound guarding a valley junction, its ivy and rubble remains little noticed nowadays[1].

*   *   *

Some five miles to the east of the border ridge, a little off the main Hereford to Abergavenny road, and sitting in the middle of gently rolling and prosperous farming countryside with its black-and-white houses and the occasional cluster of a village, is Kilpeck. You approach the older part of the village through a rectangular area of undulating mounds, a few orchard trees, and the odd wandering cow, past a substantial building that is a hotchpotch of different ages and styles, and arrive at the village green. There is the church, and beyond it, encroached by the smoothed overspill of more recent graves, is another series of higher mounds, topped by the smallest of broken walls, like a Victorian folly, and surrounded by damp patches oozing frog-spawn.

Kilpeck church, founded AD 650 and rebuilt in 1135.

1. If the Welsh disliked their new foes, they do not seem to have been very popular with the people of Herefordshire either for, as the *Anglo-Saxon Chronicle* remarked in its entry for 1048, the Normans

   'inflicted all the injuries and insults they possibly could on the King's men in that region.'

   They must have been relieved when, in an odd note to history, some of those Frenchmen went off to Scotland to help Macbeth fight his battles.

Value £4 says the Domesday Book, and that was quite a large sum in Norman times. Sitting under the yews in the churchyard, there is nothing obvious to suggest the early Norman importance of the place (the present church was built later) until you climb the mound and gaze out from the top beside the broken wall. Here, the grey ridge slams the horizon shut, and to the northeast, about the same distance away, a haze above a curve of the Wye announces the unseen presence of Hereford. For Kilpeck was a Norman border village, a military outpost of Hereford, and the mound on which you are standing is one of those that the Welsh watchers would have seen being erected along the border at the end of 1066 and the beginning of 1067.

By then Hereford was more than just a town. It was one of the strategic centres of western Britain, the buffer between Wales and the fertile lands of Mercia and the west Midlands. It had been fortified as early as the 8th century, and King Offa had run his dyke dividing Mercia from Wales just beyond it[2]. It also stood at the north of an area open to the plundering of swift raiders swooping up the Severn, the Wye or the Usk. William, trying to secure his borders whilst imposing Norman rule behind them, despatched his closest associate, William FitzOsbern, to be Earl of Hereford with the almost independent powers that the king was careful to deny his barons elsewhere and which were paralleled only on the northern border. The Hereford men had an obligation to follow the Sheriff on any expedition into Wales, and anyone failing to fulfill this duty was fined 40s.

The Domesday Book ranks Hereford as a 'city', one of only 16 in England. The word 'city' hardly signifies the kind of urban area we imagine today, but it was still a substantial conglomeration of people. Domesday lists '103 men dwelling inside and outside the wall' belonging directly to the king, and another 98 dwellings (later falling to 60) held by the Bishop of Hereford. This figure has to be multiplied by all those dependents living with the men, plus the addition of those in whom the Book was not interested and did not record: the total population figure may have been between 700 and 1,000[3]. The main rents were $7\frac{1}{2}$d from each house (plus 4d for hire of horses) inside the walls, and $3\frac{1}{2}$d outside, and the main obligations were military service, although

> 'on three days in August [every household] reaped at Marden [a royal manor], and on one day had to gather hay where the Sheriff wished.'

2. Contrary to popular myth, Offa's Dyke was a grand boundary ditch marking the border rather than a defensive wall.
3. This figure is very much speculative. By comparison, in 1086 Lincoln, Norwich, Oxford and York may have had between 4,000 and 5,000 people (York was down from a pre-Conquest figure of about 9,000), and a scattering of towns such as Bury St. Edmunds, Canterbury, Exeter and Wallingford about 2,000. The populations of the two major centres of London and Winchester are unknown, but the former may have been as large as York. The total population of England was probably between $1\frac{1}{2}$ million and 2 million, though it has been the subject of much inconclusive debate.

Ownership of horses seems to have been particularly important, and the population included six smiths, each of whom had to make 120 horseshoes a year out of the king's own iron, for which they were paid 3d, and who were exempt from any other service. There appears to have been a market, and there was certainly a mint, with seven moneyers. Aethelstan's cathedral had been restored, (to be replaced by the present Norman building, started around 1080) and there was a nunnery. For royal visits a King's Hall was maintained, and escort duty for the royal court was provided by the citizens.

Outside the city, as this was a prime area for any foreign leader wishing to take advantage of the uncertain situation following the Conquest, and the Normans were vastly outnumbered by the indigenous population (not to mention the Welsh), one of the first considerations was the establishment of border castles. They were of necessity more modest affairs than the giant stone-walled, multi-towered edifices that still dominate so much of our national heritage. The main point of defence was a large earth mound, the motte, on top of which was the main wooden keep or fortified tower; in some cases the tower seems to have been built first on stilts, and the earth mound then thrown up around it. The top of the tower made a suitable watching-point, the steep sides of the mound and the tower itself an easily defended strongpoint. A site near a stream was advantageous, as its waters could be diverted to form a moat around the motte as an extra defence and as a water supply. To one side of the mound stretched an oval of an earthwork, tracing a path rather like a comet around the sun, and enclosing a flat open area – the bailey. Here would be any domestic buildings, and a space where villagers and their animals could retreat in times of danger. A second moat usually surrounded the bailey, whose earthworks were surmounted by their own wooden stockade.

The advantage of this simple system was that the position could easily be held by a small number of men. Equally important, it could be built in a very short space of time (four days for the motte) with local, press-ganged labour. In building the castles those English labourers were putting the seal on their own submission to the Normans, for not only were they defensive fortresses, they also dominated the surrounding land with their military superiority. The sight of the wooden tower on top of the earthen mound must have been a daily reminder of the consequences of the Conquest, unparalleled by any Anglo-Saxon lordly building.

*   *   *

Some 3,000 motte-and-bailey castles have left their traces in Britain, and Herefordshire is one of the best places to see them. They turn up in the crook of a stream or on the edge of a village; the tell-tale mound covered with a copse of trees, substantial enough to be left alone by ploughing farmers. The mound at Kilpeck was such a castle, and among the brambles, the gravestones, and the little terraces formed by sheep-paths rather than any human agency, one can easily trace the basic outlines. It was presumably built by William FitzNorman, who held it directly from the king (as opposed to being a sub-tenant of one of the major landholders), and who was one of a number of second-ranking Normans holding similar responsible positions on the border. His motte-and-bailey served as his administrative centre, and his bailey must have been the scene of local events as well as a refuge in times of strife.

The Kilpeck site seems to have been a defensive position under the Anglo-Saxon regime. Behind the church to the east is that rectangular area raised a little from the surrounding land and filled with the undulations of former occupation. This was a fortified Saxon village, whose houses nestled in orderly fashion within the defensive earthworks, and whose western fortifications were probably incorporated into the Norman construction[4]. What state these defences were in when William FitzNorman took over, and how thriving the village was, we have no way of knowing. However, the very large number of men mentioned in the Domesday entry – 61 men with 19 ploughs, although this may represent an area extending well beyond the village itself – and the constant warfare of the preceding period, suggests that Kilpeck was very much a going concern, a small town rather than a village.

The Domesday Book provides some clues to the nature of the place, though, as so often, they are shrouded in uncertainty. The general situation in England was that communities consisted of a number of men working directly for the lord and his manorial home-farm, a number who did service on the lord's land but also farmed their own, and a number who were relatively free of obligation. The proportions varied widely, and the resulting pattern of village life is dealt with at greater length when we come to Newton Bromswold.

However, such a relationship between manor and villagers was less clearly defined along the Welsh border. Whereas Anglo-Saxon society had been moving towards a manorial and feudal system, Celtic tradition was not so advanced, and this was an area with a strong Celtic influence. The ties between manor and village were largely based on arable agriculture; it was less easy to impose rent or service on a pastoral society, and the Marches must have contained a high proportion of sheep-farming, as they still do. In addition, living in an area that was constantly fought over and regularly in danger must have bred a high degree of independence[5]. Kilpeck seems

4. The rectangular shape and the layout of the scant remains resemble Newton Bromswold (q.v.)
5. There was a similar situation in East Anglia, where the combination of a Danish smallholding tradition and the threat of Scandinavian invasions or raids led to an independence that resisted the imposition of manors and the social relationships they implied.

to bear this out, for there is little suggestion of an all-dominant home-farm. It had three ploughs, the great plough normally drawn by eight oxen, and this was the standard measure of arable productivity in Domesday England. Presumably there were six men to operate them, two to each plough team, and these may have included the four ploughmen mentioned in the entry as *bovari*, a word that usually implied servile status.

William FitzNorman also had two slaves, whose position was much as the name implies. These two (and Domesday does not record their sex or their function) could have been cook and seamstress or ploughman or baker, and may have ended up as slaves for a number of reasons. Most likely they were captured in battle or during a foray into Wales, but they could also have been the children of slaves, or have been thrown into slavery as a punishment for a crime or for the inability to pay a fine. Most pathetic of all, the poor sometimes sold themselves or their children into slavery in times of famine or destruction following warfare or raids. Slaves sometimes had the right to work for themselves in their own free time, and could buy their freedom: the accepted price for a slave was £1 or the value of an eight-oxen ploughing team. Their ownership was widespread (even the Church kept large numbers) although their number seems unexpectedly low in the Welsh Marches. Either there was little tradition of keeping slaves in the area, or the Domesday Book did not record slaves acquired through the warfare with the Welsh. Their numbers fell after the Conquest, not so much from Church pressure (although some clerics disapproved of the practice) as from the pragmatic Norman way of looking at things. A slave was expensive to keep, and more to the point did not produce any profit in cash terms. It seemed more sensible to free slaves, and then take off them rent for land and their obligations of service on the manor farm.

The two Kilpeck slaves may have been the lowest of the low, but the 57 men of Kilpeck seem to have been unexpectedly free. The entry specifically states that they do no service except fulfill their obligation to fight in the army. The kind of tax they pay – 15 sesters[6] of honey and 10s – is also peculiar to the region, and is usually associated with Welsh village communities, following long-established local customs which, on the whole, the Normans preferred to leave alone. Along with the rectangular enclosure, the composition of the village strongly suggests that William FitzNorman found a busy community whose primary function was military; defence against the Welsh, a *raison d'etre* that was continued under the Norman regime. Here was something more than a village – a small town, probably the first on the road south from Hereford, for the moment the next strategic link along the border. As evidence, the traces of house platforms are faintly marked to the north of the road that runs through the raised rectangular area, and it seems a far cry from the sleepy village

6. A sester is thought to have been about 32 ounces of honey.

strung out in all directions today, giving no hint of the former importance of this local centre.

The intricate carved pillars around the doorway into Kilpeck church.

Having 61 men on whom he could immediately call if the Welsh loomed over the ridge or if Irish Vikings stormed up the valley may have been strategically advantageous to William FitzNorman, but it was not so helpful to the economy of his own agricultural holdings. Kilpeck was a small town, but doubtless some of the inhabitants had useful specialist skills on which he could draw – a falconer, a tailor, or perhaps a weaponsmith. Although FitzNorman treated Kilpeck as his *caput* (the centre of holdings and probably main place of residence), he had many other areas of land to draw on.

There were 32 landholders in Herefordshire (besides the king and the Church), all of whom had been granted their estates by King William. They included some of the great men of the country who had land all over Britain – Alfred of Marlborough, Hugh Donkey, Urso of Abetot. FitzNorman was no great magnate, although he was typical of the second tier of those who crossed the Channel with the Conquest. He had parcels of land dotted all over the immediate region: a couple around Leominster, another near Ross-on-Wye, and two straddling a bend on the Wye. The patchwork nature of his holdings was echoed by those of other landholders; Anglo-Saxon lords, less overtly concerned with the profit of property, had owned a piece of land here, another there, and the Norman lords, being granted the property of individual Anglo-Saxons, inherited the system. After the battle of Hastings this system proved to be extremely advantageous to King William, because it prevented the barons from accumulating too much power at a time of transition by using a large swathe of land as a power-base.

William FitzNorman's other lands were quite different from Kilpeck in social composition. His northernmost holding, Broadward, for example, included:

'$\frac{1}{2}$ hide[7]. In lordship 1 plough; 2 villagers, a smith and 5 smallholders with 2 ploughs. 2 slaves; a mill at 10s; a fishery at 500 eels. The value was 20s; now 30s.'

From here his table could be supplied with that medieval staple diet, eels, which abounded in the streams and ponds that served the mills. This holding was also a thriving one, for it had increased its value, and therefore its productivity, by 50 per cent between the Conquest and the compilation of the Domesday Book. He had sub-let some of his lands, such as Hopton; the Vern had been held by two *radmen*, 'riding-men', whose duties included escort work and the conveying of goods before 1066. The general picture is one of an increase in prosperity; but Domesday sounds an accountant's note in its entry for Munsley:

'$\frac{1}{2}$ plough more would be possible there'

which would mean, of course, more tax for the king.

---

7. A hide was a unit of land, ostensibly 120 acres, used as a measure of tax assessment.

What the Kilpeck ploughman would have seen, looking across to Wales, were not the rolling fields of today. Domesday makes little mention of any villages in this quite extensive area, apart from a couple of outlying settlements that seem to have been as much Welsh as Norman. It was, in fact, a wasteland, where any holdings had probably been devastated in the warfare of the earlier part of the century. It was known as Archenfield and there is evidence to suggest that much of it was forested, or at least thicketed uncultivated land, an adjunct to the Forest of Dean to the south. Such country would provide a buttress to the border villages, a no man's land before Wales. Those who did live in this area seem to have followed Welsh custom rather than any Anglo-Saxon or Norman system. Under this tradition, for example, if a Welshman stole

'a man, a woman, a horse, an ox or a cow, when he is convicted of it, he first restores what he stole.'

This was an idea outside the Norman laws, which preferred compensation to restoration. The Welsh concept of family vendetta is reminiscent of an earlier age:

'But if a Welshman has killed a Welshman, the relatives of the slain man gather and despoil the killer and his relatives and burn their homes until the body of the dead man is buried the next day about midday. The King has a third part of this plunder, but they have all the rest free.'

If an Englishman killed an Englishman, he could expect a heavy fine, or at the worst mutilation, but that would have been the end of the matter.

The forest itself had a purpose for the Normans: it was a royal hunting-ground for the favourite pastime of the Norman kings. As the Domesday Book relates:

'When the King was engaged in hunting, by custom one man from each and every house [in Hereford] went to stall game in the woodland.'

William was just as likely to have hunted in Archenfield as further to the north, where the 'Hay' in Hay-on-Wye, up the river from Hereford, refers to the enclosure into which the game were driven for capture, a living reminder of those joys of the chase[8]. The inhabitants of Archenfield had obligations directly related to this sport: the villeins of Treville wood (between Kilpeck and Kingstone) took venison to Hereford as their only service. William FitzNorman himself seems to have had some sort of responsibility for supervising the royal hunting-grounds of the Forest of Dean, although no details of his obligations or duties survive. He was described as 'the forester of Herefordshire', and certainly he rented forest areas off the king (who was

8. A fuller description of the Norman forest and its harsh laws will be found in the chapter on Savernake Forest. The area under Forest Law around Hay actually extended into the city of Hereford itself.

not above letting his royal forests out if there was money in it) for £15. Much of Treville wood still remains; presumably FitzNorman thought he could make a profit out of it, and the trees to be seen there today may be the direct descendants of those of his age.

*   *   *

As it happened, William FitzNorman did not have to worry about the Welsh, even if tension, mistrust, and uncertainty remained. Potential turmoil had threatened in 1075 when Roger, Earl of Hereford, who succeeded his father in 1071, unsuccessfully rebelled against the king, thus forfeiting his lands and his title. But there seems to have been little local support for this insurrection, and Herefordshire avoided the royal devastation that Yorkshire and the North suffered after a similar revolt. Across the border, the Welsh kings had warred among themselves and, in 1081, William the Conqueror led a Norman expedition into South Wales. At St David's he met Rhys ab Owain, and helped restore him to his kingdom of Deheubarth; in return Rhys paid him £40 a year as a vassal king, thus pacifying the border.

Indeed, shortly after the compilation of the Domesday Book, the Normans moved westwards up the valley past Hay, building castles at Hay, Bronllys, and Talgarth in 1088. A similar movement occurred up the Usk valley westwards from Abergavenny; soon the Black Mountains were surrounded and placed under Norman control, although still subject to ambush or guerilla attack. The whole length of the ridge facing Kilpeck was therefore no longer an immediate threat, apart from the occasional hiccup such as the Welsh raid in 1093 when Rhys, forgetting his subservience to the Normans, was killed. As the border moved westwards, so the Church followed, and the lovely Llanthony Priory was founded in the middle of the mountains as an Augustinian house in 1107.

There was, of course, a church at Kilpeck, and one of considerable antiquity. Hereford had had a cathedral since the 8th century, but the Kilpeck foundation was older: it is recorded that it and its lands were given to the Welsh diocese of Llandaff (Cardiff) around 650. William FitzNorman would not have found the present Norman church, but a Saxon structure, and some of this building remains, incorporated into the fabric of the later building. But it is the Norman church itself that immediately catches the eye, not the long and short work of the Saxon buttress quoins in the northwest corner of the chancel[9]. It is perhaps the most beautiful, and certainly the most extraordinary, small church in Britain, its red sandstone always

9. Quoins are the squared stones at the corners of a building. Long and short work is the method of arranging quoins that is characteristic of Saxon building methods. In the most distinctive arrangement, a large quoin was placed vertically on top of a quoin placed horizontally, and so on up the corner of the wall.

glowing a gentle-pink. It boasts an apology for a tower. Above the main door is set a jagged semi-circle, like grinning teeth, topped by a row of nightmarish, grotesque faces. Serpentine figures twine around the pillars, and all around the church under the eaves a series of sculptures glare down: a badger, a dog, a musician playing a fiddle, strange emasculated babies, even a woman who seems to be all too obviously offering herself to the upturned gaze of the onlooker. The carver of this riot of ideas and imagery had started at nearby Shobden church, now in ruins, built by Oliver de Merlimond following a pilgrimage to Santiago de Compostela. Undoubtedly, de Merlimond had been impressed by the mass of decorative sculpture at the Spanish cathedral, a concept not found in such profusion in Saxon or Norman churches, and had wished to emulate something of the same effect in his corner of England. Shobden certainly impressed William FitzNorman's grandson Hugh, who around 1135 had the time and the security to rebuild the church at Kilpeck, and hired the same artisan to decorate it.

Two of the carved stone beasts under the eaves of Kilpeck church.

The idea of a wealth of stone carving may have been inspired by an Iberian cathedral, but the style is anything but Spanish. The figures breathe the spirit of the old Celtic religions; of the dark side of the subconscious, of the beasts that wandered through the forests. Although they are later than Domesday, they must represent the kind of experience and outlook that the Normans encountered among the indigenous population when they arrived: a kind of visual record of the way men looked at the world, and of the conglomeration of the cultures that they had inherited, and nothing quite like it exists outside the area.

The shades of the Vikings stalk here, in the serpentine heads that gape out from the west side, and in the intricate intertwining of the pillars of the door, like 10th-century jewellery transformed into stone. From some folk memory of the Dark Ages come little manikin figures with huge round, staring eyes, sometimes being gobbled up by a fearsome beast; monsters that must have haunted children in the night leer down with bestial faces. In happier imagery, the fiddler scrapes away, recalling music and festivities; an imposing ram smiles down with self-satisfaction, knowing he is about to go among the ewes. Everywhere there are images of the hunt, quite clearly the carver's response to a particular FitzNorman interest. A hare lies beside a dog. A badger looks out alert, wondering whether to be bold and attack or be sensible and retreat. The sport of kings, the stag, runs under the roof, and a bird of prey stands ready to be let loose on its quarry.

Here and there are also religious images more directly influenced by Spanish models: pillars of saints inside the church, and what may be a lamb with a cross, the symbol of pilgrimage, outside. The English Church had long been promoting the veneration of saints as a Christian counterpart to the worship of spirits, and had gradually fostered the idea of nature as something alien from man and God, the province of devils and evil spirits. But such teachings do not seem to have permeated through to Kilpeck; here in these carvings is an older tradition, an understanding of nature and its ways, almost a memorial to the spirits of the forest creatures. Being a culture in transition, the evilness of some of the carved beasts is tempered by the intercession of the saints; but there is a hint inside the church that the carver was working with a long collective memory. By the chancel there is a curious font that is Saxon, not Norman; it looks rather like the belly of a portly and sagging gentleman, his two feet peeping out at the base, his hands firmly clasped around his waistline, as if trying to hold it in. There is something fanciful and grotesque about it, a forerunner of the carvings that surround it.

One can speculate endlessly on the allegorical messages of all these figures, for no one has satisfactorily explained them, if indeed they are allegorical. But undoubtedly one is in the presence of an imagination nurtured by the centuries preceding the Conquest, and which was to be almost entirely erased in the centuries to follow. Kilpeck itself had its later moments of glory: a small stone castle replaced the wooden structure, and there William de Cantilupe, a great border baron, entertained King John a number of times. A small Benedictine priory, of which virtually nothing remains, was established a few hundred yards to the east of the church. Of the atmosphere of that later history not a jot greets the modern visitor; what endures is a memorial to the times when the Normans first took over. It was left to a forgotten stone-carver to bequeath images of hunts through forests, of the dreams and realities of a village swept over by the Celts, the Vikings, and now the Normans. To feel a combination of militarism, uncertainty, and the continuity of tradition and culture, and, indeed, the paradoxical orderliness of the times, one could hardly start at a better place than the apparently sleepy village of Kilpeck.

Traveller's Guide

Location of Kilpeck

SO 446305 (metric map 148; 1-inch map 142). From Hereford (7 miles) south on A465, from Abergavenny (17 miles) north on A465. Kilpeck is signposted off the main road, 2 miles down country lanes.

Other local Anglo-Saxon sites

Ewyas Harold SO 384287: remains of pre-Conquest motte-and-bailey castle.

Other local Norman sites

Motte-and-bailey castles sites: Of the many in the area, there is a good isolated example at **Didley (SO 451320)** a mile to the north of Kilpeck; a haunting, marsh-surrounded mound at **Orcop (SO473266)** to the south-east, and another at **Longtown** (see below).

The Herefordshire school of sculpture: This is the title given to the style of carving, of which Kilpeck is the most complete example. Others will be found at **Aston Eyre (SO 655940), Brinsop (SO 442448), Castle Frome (SO 665459), Chaddesley Corbett (SO 891736), Eardisley (SO 312491), Fownhope (SO 581343), Rock (SO 731711), Rowlstone (SO 374270), Stottesdon (SO 672829)** and **Stretton Sugwas (SO 460420)** churches, **Leominster Priory (SO 498593)** and in the ruins of **Shobden church**, re-erected as a folly in the grounds of **Shobden Court (SO 401629)**.

Hereford: Castle ruins, town walls, etc.

Garway SO 455224: Knights Templar church and dovecote.

Grosmont SO 406245: Ruins of castle.

Llanthony SO 288278: Ruins of Augustinian priory in beautiful surroundings.

Longtown SO 321291: Ruins of castle; earlier motte-and-bailey to south of town.

Skenfrith SO 457202: Interesting castle with square-plan outer walls and round keep.

White Castle SO 379168: Marvellous and beautiful castle in isolated position with spectacular moat and fortified outer bailey.

Interesting border village sites elsewhere in England and Wales

Elsdon, Northumberland NY 937935 (metric map 81; 1-inch map 77). Motte-and-bailey castle c 1066 in lonely and wild area near border between England and Scotland, with associated village (and early village green).

More, Shropshire SO 340915 (metric map 137; 1-inch map 129). Ringwork castle, and the remains of ditched and enclosed village; (the newer replacement village is situated around the church on higher ground).

Skipsea, Humberside TA 163551 (metric map 107; 1-inch map 99). Huge motte-and-bailey castle defending the coast against Scandinavian invasion and raids.

Tomen-y-Rhodwydd, nr. Llandegla, Clwyd SJ 177516 (metric map 116; 1-inch map 108). Motte-and-bailey border castle, perhaps built by the Welsh rather than the Normans.

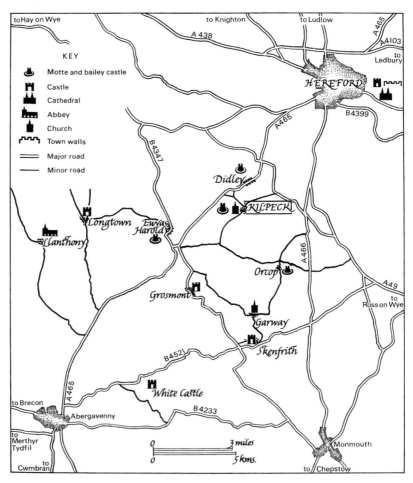

DEERHURST

A Domesday estate

ECCIA S PETRI WESTMONAST. TEN DER-
HESTE. Ibi funt. LIX. hidae. Ibi. VI ferui . . .

The Church of ST PETER'S, WESTMINS-
TER, holds Deerhurst. There are 59 hides
there. In the head of the manor there were 5
hides in the reign of King Edward. There are 3
ploughs, 20 villagers and 8 smallholders there,
with 10 ploughs. There are 6 slaves, and 60 acres
of meadow. Woodland 2 leagues long by $\frac{1}{2}$ league
wide. It was and is valued at £10.

Far away to the east of Kilpeck, ruptured by the modern conglomerations of
Gloucester and Cheltenham, lies a different landscape. Moulded around the
vicissitudes of the River Severn, the natural landmarks are distant: the warm outlines
of the Malvern Hills to the north, the edge of the Cotswolds to the east, Hay Bluff on
a clear day to the west, and hillocks and undulations nearby.

There is something haunted about this landscape. The mighty river seems hidden
from view; villages are fortified by the density of trees not only from the floods of the
Severn, but from prying eyes. Great farms hog the hilltops, looking inwards to their
central yards, the surrounding buildings windowless to the outside world; great
houses, sometimes Tudor, sometimes Georgian, often on Norman sites, are shuttered by privacy notice-boards. It is not an area that seems naturally open to the
public.

It feels ancient now, mapped out by the continuity of man. It was ancient when the
Normans arrived, and perhaps not so alien to them, familiar as they were with the
meandering Seine as it reached the sea. One of the places they must have made for,
to consolidate their hold on this rich and fertile land, was what is now a little
Gloucestershire village, masked by its screen of trees: Deerhurst, 'the wood
frequented by deer'.

Much of what can be seen today in the beautiful church and the little chapel
nearby would have greeted the Normans, for it was then an ecclesiastical centre of
great wealth and importance, if already past its prime. Its long history had been

punctuated from time to time by stirring events; the earliest parts of the church are 7th century or earlier, and it was then, some 400 years before the Conquest, probably the centre for Celtic Christianity in the kingdom of Hwicce which spanned the lower Severn Valley. Hwicce became absorbed into Mercia, its kings became earls, and the Celtic Church adopted the hierarchies of Rome. The son of one of those earls, Aethelric, was responsible for the large holdings that Deerhurst commanded when the Normans arrived, and he must have been a man of considerable substance, for in 804 he endowed Deerhurst with the staggering area of 30,000 acres, while insisting that in return he would be buried in the church.

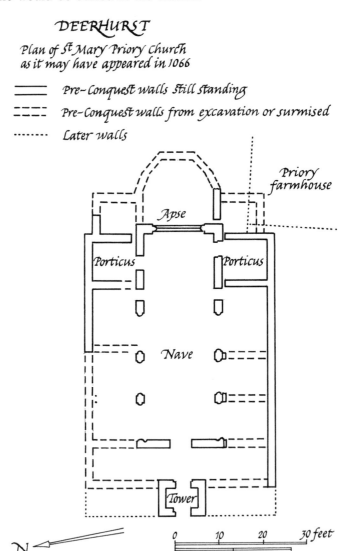

DEERHURST

Plan of St Mary Priory Church
as it may have appeared in 1066

▬▬▬   Pre-Conquest walls still standing
▬ ▬ ▬   Pre-Conquest walls from excavation or surmised
· · · · · ·   Later walls

Then suddenly in 1016, not so long before the Conquest, Deerhurst found itself in the centre of British history, if just for a fleeting moment. The English king Aethelred and his son Edmund had been trying to stem the invasions of the Danes, led by Cnut, better known to later generations as Canute. On St George's Day Aethelred died, and Edmund had not long succeeded to the crown when he was decisively defeated by Cnut at Ashingdon in Essex, where, in the words of the *Anglo-Saxon Chronicle:* 'among the slain . . . were all the flower of England.' Edmund rapidly retreated to Gloucestershire, pursued by Cnut. Their mutual advisers suggested that they should meet and try to come to some sort of accommodation. Meet they did, on the neutral territory of an island in the Severn, Alney (now down beside the northern bypass around Gloucester). The Chronicle describes Alney as being 'near Deerhurst', not only showing that its writer expected his readers to have heard of the place, but tempting one to speculate that Edmund, his advisers, and the tattered remains of his army holed up there, anxiously awaiting the outcome of the meeting as Cnut rowed triumphantly up the Severn with his long-ships.

In the event the two kings:

> 'became comrades and sworn brothers, and made a compact both with pledge and also with oaths, and fixed the amount of money to be paid to the [Danish] host, and then dispersed.'

Yet again the kingdom was divided; Edmund keeping Wessex and Cnut the 'country to the north'. By the end of the year Edmund was dead, and the Dane Cnut had taken over the whole of the kingdom.

In 1066 there was probably no one left alive in Deerhurst who could recall these events, but William the Conqueror would have been well aware of what went on at Alney. His great-aunt, Emma, had married first Aethelred, and then King Cnut after he had taken over the whole of England. She thus linked the Norman Dukedom with both English and Anglo-Danish royal houses, and William unconvincingly used this rather tangled web of relationships to justify in part his claim to the English throne, and therefore legitimise his conquest.

*   *   *

Other Normans probably knew about Deerhurst, for between 1016 and 1066 it had formed close links with the Continent, though with France rather than Normandy. It had been under the overall control of St Peter's church, Westminster, until Edward the Confessor invited Baldwin, a monk of St Denis' church in Paris, to become Prior of Deerhurst. When Baldwin left to be Abbot of Bury St. Edmunds in 1065, Edward divided the large estate, giving much of the land to the Parisian church: as clear an example as any of the kind of cross-channel links that were well

37

established before the Conquest, although one wonders whether Baldwin was invited because he was a good prelate, or because he was also Edward the Confessor's doctor. Whatever the reason, William the Conqueror confirmed these arrangements, and on April 13th 1069, transferred the actual church at Deerhurst to the control of St Denis.

The church building that witnessed this history is, in spite of later additions, quite different in tone from the mass of churches that populate the British landscape, though it must have been typical of the larger pre-Conquest churches and minsters. It feels tall, thin, and gaunt, an aesthetic alien to the squat, familiar Norman parish churches, or the breadth and space of the later cathedrals. Indeed, it *is* different, for its geometry belongs to a different way of viewing the world to that which dominated the later Middle Ages. Rectangles, triangles, and half-circles create the impact, and are kept separate from each other. Nowhere, in the surviving Saxon parts of the church, is found that visual complication and interaction of forms created by the ribbed vault, or the pointed arch, or the flow of buttress into parabola.

Deerhurst church.

How much this simplicity of form was determined by taste, and how much by the constraints of building methods, there is no sure way of telling. The core of the church[1] lifts up towards God, but its narrowness is dependent on the one-storey

1. The following description refers to the church as the Normans would have found it; or, indeed, much as we can see it today.

building that preceded it because the Anglo-Saxons had no way of spanning a roof in stone, and their carpentry techniques limited the potential width of a roof. Similarly, the gentle rounded arches over the west doors, or their massive correspondent (now walled up) in the east end, reached the limits of Anglo-Saxon structural integrity; but they replaced the flat-topped doors of the earlier church, still to be seen in the choir. No such considerations affected the beautiful west double window, high on the third storey of a wall that is now on the inside of the church, for it had been faced by the top of the tower in the period before the Conquest. Its tall and narrow openings match the proportions of the nave; the balance of its fluted columns is topped by two tall triangular hoods, and the effect of scale and shape is very pleasing[2]. Similarly, the label stops – the stones that support the bottom of the curved arches, jutting out – may provide a structural purpose, but their decoration belongs to the spirit: the long, pointed dog heads, a mythical semi-Scandinavian beast. Outside is a decoration without structural intent; the Deerhurst Angel, looking as if an illustration from an illuminated manuscript had been encased in stone, and probably once one of a set of such carvings. The font twists and twines around its simple shape, decorated with trumpet spirals of Celtic inspiration, and vine scrolls of Northumbrian influence.

The very stones with which the church is made seem different. That it was made of stone at all would have made it stand out in the Anglo-Saxon landscape, for almost all buildings other than those of the Church were then made out of wood. But the Church needed more lasting buildings to emphasise the permanence of God, and to survive the prevalent danger of fire, which is one reason why the Normans developed the vaulted stone roof. At Deerhurst the oldest stones seem like a jigsaw puzzle of cobbles in their attempt at regularity, and if the upper stories of the Saxon tower use, of necessity, great corner stones, all over the church can be found the zigzag interruptions of herring-bone pattern, unexpectedly delicate, and with one course of stones laid diagonally over another of the opposite diagonal, reiterating the theme of triangles.

You have to strip away the more modern side aisles to see the church as the Normans found it, but the only major feature that is missing is the semi-circular apse, now delineated by a curve of excavated stones. Yet two aspects have to be filled in by the imagination. The first is that the carvings, and probably the interior walls, were painted, and the effect must have been totally different to the warmth of stone and simple plaster. There is no accurate way of knowing what this looked like, even if fragments of paint do survive, and for the colours and the motifs you have to turn to the pages of the illuminated manuscripts of the period. The second is that the interior space of the church would have been quite different. The central nave was

2. It may be made of reused Roman stones (there is evidence of Roman occupation in the area). There is a puzzle over this window: the only similar window seems to be in a monastery in Abyssinia.

flanked by two porticus[3] (the arch of one can still be seen) occupying the place of the transcepts of a Norman church. But in the latter, there is space between the transcepts and the nave. Here, the join is that of a solid wall; add the base of the tower, and the church is divided up into individual areas. In addition, at various times of its earlier history, the vertical layers of the church were formed by storeys, further dividing the space into portions, and explaining why doors seem to appear half-way up walls and go nowhere. Each of these areas was probably the equivalent of a chapel to an individual saint, those intermediaries between man and God. But it must have given an enclosed, monastic feel to the place (and, remember, this was the priory church), and its spirit must have been inward-looking, contemplative, quite different to the vision of the majesty, power, and self-confident display of a Norman building. Not very far away there is evidence that the Normans found this altogether too meagre and self-deprecating. For at Tewkesbury in 1121 the Norman Abbey was finished, eclipsing any vestige of importance that Deerhurst retained. There the massive tower, with its mixture of military spirit and Romanesque detail, the vast interior space and the intricate vaulting roof, could hardly be more in contrast to the simplicity of Deerhurst, or a more potent testimony to the change of regime.

*   *   *

Of the monastic buildings, nothing remains, for the house that now abuts the church formed part of later cloisters, and the bumps and ridges in the fields beyond are the sole evidence of other later buildings. The only tantalising glimpse that survives is a single column in the cellars of the house, holding up the roof in the middle of the space. Deerhurst bumbled on as a monastery until the Dissolution, but in the meantime its lands were given to Eton College in 1440, and ironically it became a cell of Tewkesbury Abbey in 1469.

The Domesday Book does not even mention the church, for the valid reason that it was not interested in ecclesiastical buildings, but in revenue and landholdings. It was therefore very interested in the estates that belonged to the church, divided up between Westminster and Paris. The relevant entries are full of detail, but because of the emphasis on the overall content of an estate and its revenue position, subject to exactly the kind of limitations that have made the Domesday Book such a difficult – or unreliable – source for the reconstruction of an immediate area. Westminster

3. A porticus (the word is used for both the singular and the plural) is a structure joining onto the main body of the church often containing a side-chapel or a burial (for burials were forbidden in the main part of the church). One characteristic shape, especially where added to a tower, is of a large porch-like structure with a pitched roof. The difference here between the porticus and Norman transcepts is that the latter were a structural part of the building, while the former were additions, and (as often happened) could be removed without risk to the main body of the church.

holds 59 hides, and Paris 60 hides, nominally over 13,000 acres, but whereas some of the lands are in the immediate vicinity, others are miles away in different counties. St Denis, Paris, even had under its tax control burgesses (townspeople) in Gloucester and Winchcombe to the northeast of Cheltenham, who owed dues to the Deerhurst Hundred. It lists the villagers, the slaves, the mills, and the water-meadows, but lumps them altogether, making it very difficult to place what went where. What one can tell, though, is the content immediately around the church. There must have been a sizable village or community, for on its five hides were 20 villagers, 8 smallholders, and 6 slaves. With the lands around the Severn (which may have followed a different course across the valley from that seen today) there was plenty of meadowland; 60 acres which were important for sheep, for general grazing, and for the provision of winter feed for stock. Finally there was woodland, 2 leagues (perhaps 3 miles) long by $\frac{1}{2}$ league ($\frac{3}{4}$ mile) wide to provide timber and pasturage for swine.

The Anglo-Saxon double pointed window in the west wall of Deerhurst church. The blocked doorway underneath once led to an upper level.

41

Domesday does list where the outlying holdings of the estate lie, sometimes directly administered, sometimes sub-let, and to wander around them is a fascinating experience, not just to glean bits of the 11th-century landscape, but also because it is a journey through rural history after the Conquest. Great roads bisect it, canals run off the Severn, and everywhere there are buildings of every age, size, and importance, constructed from every type of material, huddled around hamlets, dominating open spaces, or strung along roads. Much has to be pared away to find any Saxon core; but conversely some of the much later features are found where they are precisely because there was once a settlement of the Deerhurst estate there.

Many of these outlying cultivated areas have names that reflect earlier invasion and settlement: Elmstone, 'the place where Ealhmund's people live', Uckington, 'that of Ucca's people'. Others reflect aspects of the topography: Hardwicke, the '*wic* for the flock' or in other words a sheep farm, Tirley, a 'round glade', Wightfield, 'a field raised up above its surroundings', as it is indeed above the flood-plain of the Severn. As many of these places are a good walking distance from Deerhurst, you might reasonably expect to find churches. Churches there are, but without exception they seem to date from the 12th century, and not earlier. That at Elmstone Hardwicke, between Deerhurst and Cheltenham, may provide the answer, for in the nave stands a Saxon stone with carvings similar to the Deerhurst font that may have been the base of a Saxon cross. If so, many of the settlements may have had such a cross where people would have met, and where a priest from Deerhurst would have held an open-air service, the churches being built later when there was enough private or communal sponsorship to pay for a permanent building.

In such a landscape, devoid of church towers, that at Deerhurst would have been all the more imposing. But if the churches appear later, the villages that contain them are the direct descendants of their Anglo-Saxon equivalents listed in the Domesday Book. Most of them are grouped around a village green, some of which have now been heavily encroached upon, and which may be Anglo-Saxon or later in origin[4]. For one of these villages, Apperley, is definitely a post-Domesday creation, some distance from the Wightfield manor mentioned in the Book, and another, Leigh, has to be a later foundation as it moved a mile or so away from its church across the fields[5]. But the rest probably represent development, rebuilding, addition, and alteration to a Saxon village or hamlet.

There is one kind of dwelling place, however, that has left a more definable mark.

4. The bounds of the village greens can be seen quite clearly, even if built upon. The buildings that surround them are a wonderful mixture, and at one corner can usually be found a grander house or farm, and the village pond.
5. The villagers did not desert their church, however. The tower was rebuilt in the 15th century, and, as a notice on the font proudly proclaims, Dick Whittington's sister-in-law was baptised here!

In many of the villages are to be found the Severn equivalent of the motte-and-bailey castles that are such a feature of the Welsh Marches, though in this case they may well be Anglo-Saxon in origin as well as Norman. They are moats, water-filled ditches surrounding a square or rectangular area of raised land, and their continued importance through subsequent ages is a reminder that they were the focal point of the wealth in the area, or of an individual manor within the estate. At Uckington, for example, the moat surrounds the house and garden of a grand 18th-century mansion, and at Wightfield it is tucked in among the buildings of a large and important farm. They were a simple and effective method of defence, if crude compared with a motte-and-bailey, a fortified house, not a castle. The moat provided an obstacle and a source of food in its fish. A wooden stockade probably ran around the water's edge, and inside would have been the wooden buildings of the most important man in the immediate vicinity. The hamlets and fields lay outside, as did the churches when they were eventually built.

Easily the most evocative place is that at Leigh, partly because the resiting of the village has left the place so unspoilt. The moat is quite deep, for the most part about 12 feet wide, and still very much water-filled. It presents one of those rare pictures of rural tranquillity: the banks tumble down, the waters scarcely murmur with movement, the lushness of waterplants occupy every point of advantage, the lilies lying across the surface, the reeds upright and thick on the edge. But it also teems with water-life, with insects scurrying across the surface, ducks quacking away the time of day, and doubtless fish pondering the murkiness of the bottom mud. It seems to cry out for little boys with their jars, and bespeckled naturalists arguing over the genus of a dragon-fly.

It encloses a rather gaunt and tall farmhouse, whose main structure has seen only recent centuries, leaving the memory of earlier ages to its foundations. It sits quite high above the moat, and above any flooding, its main door some feet above the surrounding field levels, and alongside there is enough room for a lawn, and a neat and well-stocked kitchen garden. Beyond the moat on two sides lie fields; but on the other two, in the churned-up mud of the yards, are the sheds and buildings of the dairy farm. It seems likely that this area has always been used for such a purpose, right back to medieval times, as its boundary is well defined by a very old and long-disused track and a ditch.

At the corner of the complex, where the farm drive meets the access road, is the church, showing its close association with the manor farm. Away across the broad field to the north of the church, half-hidden by the swathe of surrounding trees, can be seen the chimneys and roofs of the village that had moved, and even at this distance the vague suggestion of a curve can be discerned as the houses swing around the line of the central village green. Where the village moved from is difficult to determine; but the field to the east of the moat, now thinly dotted with fruit trees, contains traces of old mounds and bumps. As it is directly opposite the church, it would seem as good a candidate as any.

But the most evocative moment at this quiet spot is when you realise that when the Domesday Book records 'in LEIGH, 1 hide', this is almost certainly that very land, ploughed and sown 900 years ago, abutting up to the churchyard. Medieval arable farming left a characteristic pattern in the landscape: as the plough team went up and down the large, undivided field, the plough picked up the soil and threw it to one side, creating a deep and broad furrow with a rounded base, and a mound of a ridge, eroded into a rounded top, lying parallel to each other in long strips: hence the name 'ridge-and-furrow'. Almost everywhere these otherwise permanent marks across the landscape have been destroyed or obscured by later farming methods, by the enlargements of villages, by the building of walls and roads, until the characteristic rises and depressions can be picked out only by the long shadows of a summer's evening, or the highlighting of snow. Here at Leigh there are no such problems[6]. The cultivated area stretched from around the corner by the dairy farm (further confirming the antiquity of the disused track that divides it from the farmyard), and then in a long wide straight slice, past the churchyard, and along the minor access road. In the great field beside the church, edged with the paraphanalia of electric fencing, the strips have been worn down by later ploughing and by years of plodding bovine feet, but the effect can still be clearly seen. Further along the road the field has been divided into smaller areas, and the one at the end has been used as an orchard, rather than ploughed down. The fruit trees neatly stand in rows along the top of the ridge, and the steep rise and fall of the medieval arable field is laid out much as it was all those years ago.

In the medieval farming system, there were two (or sometimes three) such huge fields to a village or settlement, one of which would have lain fallow for animals to graze, or for hay for winter feed. If you are lucky enough to visit Leigh at the right time of the year, you can see an echo of that system at work in one or other of the modern sub-divisions of the field. There, left untouched for the later haymaking, wild flowers intertwine with the tall grass, all growing up to about the same level, disguising the undulations of the ground beneath. But across the field the colours change; light greens and yellows, and a greater profusion of wild flowers, alternate in strips with the darker greens of different grasses. Each band of colour represents a strip of ridge-and-furrow, the darker greens the trench, the wild flowers preferring the sunnier summits in an age-old pattern.

The hay merges with the trees of the village, and you realise that the new village

6. There is now a plough especially designed to level ridge-and-furrow fields, so one wonders how long surviving examples will last, even here in quiet Gloucestershire.

grew up merely on the other side of the open field. So it turns out that the villager had no further to go with his plough-team or his scythe than his early Norman counterpart.

*   *   *

Back at Deerhurst itself there is another building, different in tone and in kind from the church or from a moat, that has fortuitously survived the vagaries of time since its dedication on April 12th 1056. Opposite the church gate, over a wall and across a small field, can be seen a typical, if ancient, black-and-white building, known as Abbot's Court. In 1885 an enterprising clergyman, the Reverend G. Butterworth, stripped the plaster off one end of this house, and found a Saxon chapel.

The *Anglo-Saxon Chronicle* for 1053 relates:

'This same year passed away Aelfric, brother of Odda, at Deerhurst, and his body rests at Pershore.'

Earl Odda was an important character of the time, who had once commanded the fleet at Sandwich, and an inscription found in a nearby orchard in 1675 confirms that he had this chapel built to commemorate his brother[7]. The same stone records the

Abbot's Court showing the Saxon chapel of Earl Odda on the left-hand side of the building.

7. The original stone is now in the Ashmolean Museum in Oxford, but there is a copy in the chapel, along with the dedication stone of the altar.

date of the dedication, but Odda himself did not long survive the occasion. A pious man, he had become a monk at Pershore, where he died on August 31st 1056, a 'good man, pure and very noble'.

The chapel was built of stone, ensuring its permanence, and merges peaceably into the timber frames of the surviving portion of Abbot's Court, still used as a home. It is a gentle building, with a homely feel, probably not very different from the halls of the day. The current entrance door (once matched by one in the opposite wall) leads into a high, simple structure of a cell, divided from the smaller chancel by another rounded top arch. The geometry, if now overlaid in the chancel by the residue of the later domestic arrangements of the house, a couple of timber beams, and the half-remains of a fireplace, again follows the theme of half-circles and straight lines. The overall impression is one of simplicity of idea. Although in its time it may have seemed a substantial building, 20 people would make it feel crowded. The simplicity of its outside walls is hardly troubled by windows, but here, on the corners of the west end, something strange happened, akin to the mystery of the Abyssinian window. The quoins slope inwards from the base, and it has been suggested that this was to create the effect, familiar from the buildings of Ancient Greece, of entasis where the slight angle was made to offset the optical illusion of vertical walls seeming to slope outwards. If so, it does not work, for the building is altogether too modest for such conceits, and the walls quite clearly slope inwards. Somehow you feel, against the steep pitch of the roof, the half-curves and straight lines of the windows and doors, that the builders should have left well alone, and followed their own geometry, leaving such complications of the spirit to interlopers or to Normans. Perhaps, after all, that inward slope was nothing to do with entasis, but was merely a mason's error, or quite simply to ensure that the walls remained standing.

*   *   *

The understated nobility of Deerhurst church, the self-effacing memorial of Odda's chapel – such things were alien to the Norman spirit, and even by the time of Domesday they belonged to the obscurity of the past; the one to become an adjunct of Tewkesbury, the other to be covered by plaster. The way men looked at things, the way they expressed themselves in the things they made, had changed. But men must still have their daily bread, and agricultural methods change slower than the cutting edge of a mason's chisel or the span of a builder's eye. It is in those ridge-and-furrow fields, in spite of moving villages and later churches, that the continuity of Saxon into Norman, and from Norman to our own times, is most appreciated.

Traveller's Guide

Location of Deerhurst

SO 870299 (metric map 150; 1-inch map 143). Signposted off the B4213, that links the A38 Tewkesbury-Gloucester road with the A417 Ledbury-Gloucester road. Tewkesbury 5 miles, Cheltenham 8 miles, Gloucester 9 miles. Motorway access: M5 Junction 9 (no access from Junction 10) and M50 Junction 2.

Other local sites of Anglo-Saxon or early Norman interest

Newent (SO 720259): 9th-century sculptured cross-shaft and carved Crucifixion scene in Norman church

Other local later Norman sites

For the more adventurous, and for those who enjoy a more modest architecture as opposed to the spectacular or grandiose, visits to what were once the outlying holdings of Deerhurst are well worthwhile, and cover buildings of the later Norman period, notably:

Hardwicke (SO 909275): Village and green. **Elmstone Hardwicke (SO 920261):** Norman church, key obtainable from bungalow opposite. **Leigh** (moat and field system **SO 865257,** village **SO 869263**): village and green, Norman church, moat, ridge-and-furrow field system.

A little further afield, there is a spectacular moat, and Tudor great house with a Norman church, at **Birtsmorton (SO 801355),** and a splendid church with many Norman features at **Upleadon Court (SO 769270).** The Tythe Barn at **Ashleworth Court (SO 818252)** is in the care of the National Trust.

It should be borne in mind that many of these sites, especially the moats and the field systems, are private property, and should not be trespassed on.

Gloucester: Roman road, famous cathedral, Norman churches, etc.

Tewkesbury: Breathtaking Norman Abbey. Exemplary reconstruction of Norman merchant's house, town museum, etc.

In addition, there are a series of churches with famous Norman sculpture, all the work of a single craftsman:

Dymock (SO 700321, Kempley (SO 665295) and **Pauntley (SO 749290).**

Interesting large Anglo-Saxon churches elsewhere in England

Barton-on-Humber, Humberside (TA 035219 metric map 112; 1-inch map 99). St Peter's church: Attractive plastered tower with stone-work copying timber structure.

Bosham, West Sussex (SU 804039 metric map 197; 1-inch map 181). Holy Trinity church with 11th-century tower and chancel arch.

Bradford-on-Avon, Wiltshire (ST 824609 metric map 173; 1-inch map 166). St Lawrence's chapel: Lower walls from 8th-century (?), upper walls 11th century in fine small Anglo-Saxon church.

Breamore, Hampshire (SU 153188 metric map 184; 1-inch map 179). The Minster Church of St Mary: Much Anglo-Saxon work and basic Anglo-Saxon structure.

Brixworth, Northamptonshire: With Deerhurst, the most famous of the surviving Anglo-Saxon churches, discussed later in this book.

Bywell, Northumberland (NZ 048615 metric map 87; 1-inch map 77). St Andrew's church: Saxon tower in now-redundant church. **NZ 049614** St Peter's church: remains of large Anglo-Saxon church incorporated in present fabric.

Earls Barton, Northamptonshire (SP 852638 metric map 152; 1-inch map 133). Famous church tower of around 1020 with elaborate stripwork decoration.

Haddiscoe, Norfolk: (TM 439969 metric map 134; 1-inch map 137). St Mary's church: Round Anglo-Saxon tower.

Haddiscoe Thorpe, Norfolk (TM 436981 metric map 134; 1-inch map 137). St Matthias' church: Round tower and 11th-century nave near Haddiscoe, above.

Hovingham, North Yorkshire (SE 666757 metric map 100; 1-inch map 92) All Saints' church: Anglo-Saxon tower and sculpture.

Lincoln Anglo-Saxon towers at St Benedict, St Peter-at-Gowts, and St Mary-le-Wigford churches, all on the High Street.

Monkwearmouth, Tyne and Wear (NZ 402577 metric map 88; 1-inch map 78). St Peter's church: 7th/11th century tall and thin tower, similar in tone to Deerhurst, and other fragmentary early remains.

Ovingham, Northumberland (NZ 085637 metric map 88; 1-inch map 78). St Mary's church: Anglo-Saxon tower.

Oxford St Michael's church, Cornmarket: Anglo-Saxon tower. **SP 513063**.

Rothwell, Lincolnshire (TF 149993 metric map 113; 1-inch map 104/5). St Mary Magdalene church: Simple but satisfying Anglo-Saxon tower.

Sompting, West Sussex (TQ 161056 metric map 198; 1-inch map 182). St Mary's church: famous for its middle 11th century 'Rheinish Helm' steeple (in the shape of a helmet), the only surviving example in Britain, and for its sculptures.

Stow, Lincolnshire (SK 882820 metric map 121; 1-inch map 104). St Mary's church: Largest Anglo-Saxon church that has survived, in cruciform plan, and much extant Anglo-Saxon material in spite of later alterations; a major monument.

Wareham, Dorset: St Martin's church: see chapter on Wareham.

Wing, Buckinghamshire (SP 880225 metric map 165; 1-inch map 146). All Saints' church: Nave and much of chancel 8th century, much rebuilt in the middle of the 10th century. Polygonal east apse, and vaulted crypt. A major pre-Conquest monument.

Worth, West Sussex (TQ 302362 metric map 187; 1-inch map 182). St Nicolas's church: Large, imposing, and important Anglo-Saxon church with rebuilt apse, whose character has survived 19th-century restoration.

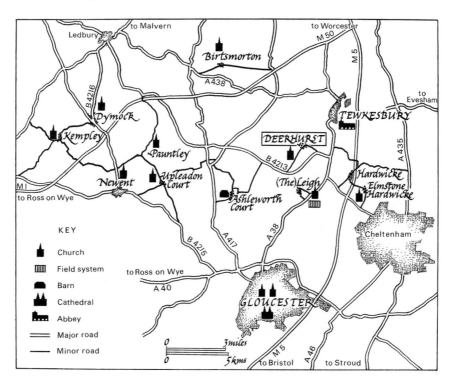

The tranquil interior of St Martin's church, Wareham.

WAREHAM

A Domesday town

In WARHAM TPR REGIS EDW erant.CXLIII
.dom. in dnio regis. . .

In WAREHAM in the reign of King Edward
there were 143 houses in the King's lordship.
This town was responsible for every service to
the king and was taxed for 10 hides – that is to
say, 1 silver mark for the King's housecarles –
besides the customary dues that belong to one
night's revenue. There were two moneyers who
each paid 1 silver mark to the King and 20s
whenever the coinage was changed. Now there
are 70 houses there – 73 have been completely
destroyed since the time of Hugh the Sheriff. In
area belonging to St Wandrille's there are 45
houses standing, and 17 are derelict. In those
areas belonging to the other barons there are 20
houses standing and 60 have been destroyed.

If you were beating down the English Channel in a small boat, driven on by an
easterly gale somewhere beyond the Isle of Wight and across the waters from
Brittany, you would come across a strange portion of the English coast. Through the
squalls you would see a long curving beach, miles in length, and lying against it the
city of Bournemouth. If you were lucky, the boat would fetch up against a narrow
entrance leading into the twists and turns, the inlets and bays, the islands of Poole
Harbour, a huge expanse of almost inland sea. If not, you would have to swing past
Durlston Head, and skirt the inhospitable cliffs of the coast of the Purbeck Hills,
looking like giant sand-dunes but actually made of the famous stone and marble,
with Lulworth Cove the main refuge. Beyond them, you would be swept against
Weymouth, the Isle of Portland, and the eerie unerring line of the pebble Chesil
Beach, with the Shambles Lightship flashing its warning to the southeast.

Safe or shipwrecked, you could take comfort in the knowledge that men had been
doing the same thing since boats first put out into the Channel. From here the
Romans went back and forth to the continent; the Vikings followed your course from

the east; the Normans put in, and the future Henry VII did not which probably saved him the crown[1]; and in Elizabethan times the fishing ships set out from Poole bound for Newfoundland and its shoals of cod.

Such thoughts have to be fuelled by the imagination, for, unlike rural Hereford-shire or Gloucestershire, where all around you can see the continuity of man, there is little on this coastline (if not inland) to prompt the historical memory. It is an area of Victorian town-building, of thirties bungalows, of retirement homes among power-station smokestacks, of the leisured concerns of an industrial, not a rural, age. The roads are crowded with queues and short tempers; the beauty spots are the dominion of ice-cream vendors, expensive car-parks, and hot and grumpy children. Even the loneliness of the Purbeck Hills is artificial, carved out by the great Army gunnery ranges, a no man's land when the red flags are flying, as they always seem to be when you visit. Yet, as always, the evidence of the past is never too far away: an old village on the road to Lulworth, a mill straddling a stream, a Norman church beside a filling-station. In the middle of this area, where Poole Harbour reaches in behind the Purbeck Hills, is a small town, easily passed by, that encapsulates an era within its modest bounds. It is a cheerful and proud place, and if half of Wareham's myriad tales are pure fiction, half of them are true. What is more, thanks to modest modern development, its late Saxon history and the feel of the town when the Normans arrived can be traced on the ground today.

* * *

If Wareham is now a lively town, it was even more so in 1066, a busy trading centre and one of the most important ports on the southern coast. Centuries earlier it had displaced Hengistbury, on the other side of Bournemouth, as the entry point for crossing the Channel, and although there were other settlements around Poole Harbour – Hamworthy, an embryonic Poole, even Bournemouth itself[2] – they were small. Wareham, as far inland as one can get using Poole Harbour, was the focal point, the centre where roads met. To the northeast, following the line of the present main road, you set out for Winchester or London, via the nunnery at Wimborne Minster, or joined the main highway through Christchurch and Lymington along the south coast. Due north there was a choice of routes, one through Lytchett Minster to Old Sarum, another through Crawford to Blandford, and yet another to Bere Regis,

---

1. In 1483 as Henry of Richmond, he saw the breakers on the shore and the large armed and hostile crowds waiting for him, and sailed on to land in Wales. Following his victory at the Battle of Bosworth Field, the Tudor dynasty was founded; had he landed here, he could well have been defeated.
2. Bournemouth is not a 19th-century foundation as is so often suggested.

now minor roads rather than major arteries. Leading to the old Roman centre of Dorchester to the west there was the already ancient high road, or the valley low road; while south you could travel to Corfe or the Purbeck Hills.

The Normans would have approached the town from the north, and as they skirted Poole Harbour they would have crossed some wild country. The area immediately around the harbour was marsh and bog, and the higher ground which the traveller used was heath or woodland; even today it is relatively sparsely

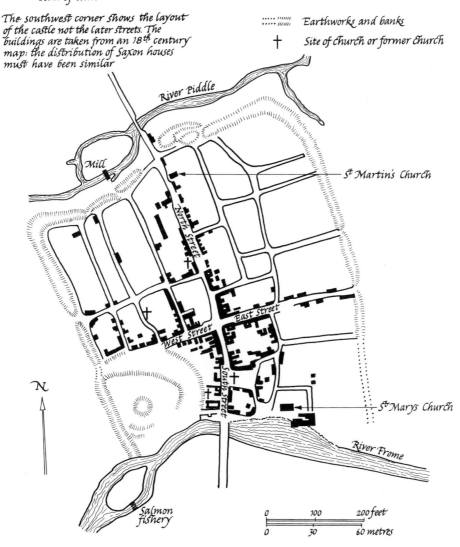

WAREHAM
Plan of town

The southwest corner shows the layout of the castle not the later streets. The buildings are taken from an 18th century map: the distribution of Saxon houses must have been similar

:::: ''''' Earthworks and banks

✝ Site of Church or former Church

River Piddle

Mill

St Martin's Church

North Street

West Street

East Street

South Street

St Mary's Church

N

River Frome

Salmon fishery

0   100   200 feet
0   30   60 metres

populated[3]. As they came down the gentle slope to Wareham itself, they were confronted by more marsh, through which meandered the little River Piddle. Even now it has a wilder feeling than its surroundings, a patch of fen country among surburbia, with marshland reeds, water-logged plants, and a tangle of trees marking out the course of the river. In 1066 it was wetter, for at high tide the sea probably covered it, and it was flooded regularly; you have to imagine a shoreline swamp, some of it bound together by hardy plants and couch-grass, ringing with the cries of wading-birds and gulls, through which ran the main channel fed by the Piddle. To the west, this estuarine scene gradually evolved into the fen and meadow of today; to the east the main body of water was a mile or so away, across some firmer land bordered by marsh[4].

Across the river was the town, but the Normans would have seen as little of it as you do today when you approach on the main road. For they were faced by a tall and formidable earthen bank, around 700 yards long, with a stone wall stretching along the top, broken in the middle by the gap of North Gate. If they were circumspect, and decided to check the lie of the land before entering the town, they would have found similar banks on the east and the west, each around 800 yards long and thus enclosing a large square. On the south side was another river, the Frome, with its own South Gate. Wareham means 'the settlement beside the weir' – not a barrage to alter the flow of the river, but a weir to trap salmon as they moved upstream, probably in long conical nets of a kind to be seen in Britain until recently. Old maps show a salmon fishery beside the island a little way up the river from the present South Bridge, and this was probably the site when the Normans completed their circuit of Wareham.

*   *   *

The southern side of the town never had an earthen bank. The river was wider and deeper than it is now, again running through marshland prone to tidal flooding, extensive and treacherous enough to be a defence in itself. For Wareham, sitting on slightly higher and firmer ground, had had a long defensive history before the Normans arrived, a promontory sticking out into Poole Harbour with the waters and bogs of the two rivers either side. Iron Age pits have been found, the spit of land was occupied in Roman times (though there was no town there then), and by the 8th century it was certainly a religious centre. When exactly the banks were built is

3. Much of this area is now coniferous forest rather than heath; but Morden Bog has been preserved as an example of bogland habitat.
4. Domesday confirms this with an entry for Bestwall, meaning 'the place east of the wall [of Wareham]'.

unclear: the west bank, cutting off the only land access, may be as old as the 7th century. King Alfred ensured that the town became a defensive stronghold in his wars with the Danes, and indeed may have had the north and east banks constructed.

By 876 the kingdom of Wessex was in trouble. The Danes had overrun East Anglia, Mercia, and Northumberland, were raiding into Scotland, and had been attacking, harrying, and raiding Wessex for a number of years. In 876 the 'host' (as the *Anglo-Saxon Chronicle* calls the Danes) took Wareham, and although they came to a solemn agreement with Alfred to leave Wessex, they comprehensively tricked him and took Exeter as well. With the limitations on movement and shortage of available food, winter was no time for warfare, and increasingly the Danes chose to set up winter quarters in Britain rather than return to Scandinavia. In the winter of 876/877 they stayed in Wareham, but as the fighting season started again they set out in their long-ships to join forces with their compatriots who had remained in Exeter.

But disaster struck. They had to round Durlston Head before sailing west, but an easterly gale must have suddenly sprung up as they were off Swanage. Viking ships could not beat against the wind if the force of the storm was stronger than their oar-power, and here they would have been caught on a classic lee shore. 120 ships were lost, peace was made, and the Danes withdrew to Mercia. Presumably Wareham was back in the hands of the men of Wessex, but not for long, for the Danes overran the kingdom again in the following year. Alfred withdrew to the Somerset marshes, reformed his forces, and regained control of his kingdom, extending it over the subsequent years and ushering in a time of stability, though at the cost of constant threat and skirmishes with the Danes.

Part of Alfred's deterrent against further invasion was to establish or restore fortified towns as focal points for defence, a policy continued in Edward's reign and whose details have survived in a document known as the *Burghal Hidage*. The majority of these strongpoints were on the Wessex coastline, and Wareham was one of them. The system was simple and comprehensive: people and livestock could retreat behind the fortifications of the *burh* when raiders threatened. To man the walls there was a quota of hides in the surrounding countryside for each fort: every hide provided one man so that there would be a soldier for every four feet. Wareham's quota was 1600 hides, which almost exactly corresponds to the length of the three walls; the responsibility for the defence of the river side was not recorded.

Alfred also refitted his navy in 897. In the words of the *Anglo-Saxon Chronicle*.

'Then King Alfred ordered warships to be built to meet the Danish ships: they were almost twice as long as the others, some had 60 oars, some more; they were both swifter, steadier, and with more freeboard than the others . . .'

It was quickly in action, probably in Poole Harbour itself. Alfred's ships blockaded the Danes inside the harbour; they beached their ships, and fighting took place on the mud-flats. Although three of the six beached ships did escape, two of them were too badly crippled to last, and the engagement was a confirmation of the potential of Alfred's new navy. This seems to have been a technological as well as a numerical improvement and it is likely that some of these ships were stationed at Wareham, so recently a target for raiders. In spite of the increased freeboard these ships were of shallow draught, easily capable of rowing up the tidal waters of the Frome. At Wareham they did not tie up at a quay; instead they were beached like modern fishing boats in an estuary. The landing-place was where the present quay and car-park are situated, for then the shoreline was slightly further back into the town just below St Mary's church. At a time of crisis, with 1600 men manning the walls, their wives and their children milling around, the ships' crews strung along the beach waiting for the order to push off, prayers being said in the nunnery, and oxen and sheep putting up a confusion of noise, Wareham must have been a crowded place.

A community, a cluster of houses, had already built up around Wareham's religious establishments and its port. But sometime between 890 and the early 11th century, perhaps even on Alfred's own general instructions, the grid plan of roads, streets, and lanes that form modern Wareham was laid out[5]. Wandering around the town today, you can still be told that the layout is Roman, but this is wishful thinking. The late 9th and 10th centuries, with their achievements in other fields – English writings, illuminated manuscripts, intellectual links with the continent – were well capable of planning a town on a grid system. Ruined Roman examples may well have prompted the idea, but other *burhs* – Wallingford, for example, or Oxford – followed a pattern similar to Wareham without Roman origins, and where Roman structures were utilised, as at Winchester or Porchester, the Saxon grid did not necessarily follow the Roman[6]. Not only did Wareham's fortress status confirm its pre-eminence in the area, but it must have created a new layer of regular work, with the banks to be maintained, the ditches to be cleared, ships to be fitted out and repaired; a grid system was well able to accommodate new town dwellers.

At the end of this period a stone wall was added to the tops of the earthen banks (only to be taken down again in the 12th century), but even such refinements could not prevent Cnut sacking the town in 1015, landing at the mouth of the Frome on his way to the heart of Dorset a year before he met Edmund at Alney. But if proof were needed of the soundness of the original conception, the banks withstood the

5. To be strictly accurate, the house frontages have moved a few feet on the main street since the 10th century; but the alignment and layout are Saxon.
6. The Saxons could have copied the concept from Roman ruins without trouble. For comparison, 400 years passed between the departure of the Romans and the creation of the *burhs*; 400 years have also passed since the Dissolution of the Monasteries, and we could copy the layout of their remains without difficulty.

onslaught of the Civil War, and the west bank was refortified as an anti-tank barrier in 1940[7].

* * *

Wareham was thus one of the first recognisable English towns since the Roman legions sailed back across the Channel for the last time and their urban creations fell into gradual decay. When the new military rulers, the Normans, rode in through the North Gate the first building they would have noticed was St Martin's church, perched up against the bank above the road[8], its stone structure a useful addition to the town's defences at a potentially weak spot. By tradition, a church had been founded here by St Aldhelm in the 670s; but this was a new building, probably constructed after Cnut's sack of the town, and its location served another useful purpose. Travellers from the north, thankful to have arrived safe and sound, would wish to make a thanksgiving offering, and there was the church waiting to receive their money before they had even set foot down the main street.

St Martin's church, Wareham, from the south.

7. One 20th-century Mayor of Wareham wanted to bulldoze the banks down, but fortunately wiser councils prevailed!
8. The Normans may however have seen a mill outside the walls where the North Mill now stands; an intriguing turn-of-the-century photograph shows an early thatched building, now destroyed, that suggests a continuity of site.

The church is much as it was then, apart from the tall Norman porch and south aisle, and later alterations to interior and window detail. There is still an air of tranquillity in the simple structure, with its rectangular nave and smaller rectangular chancel, a sense of a peaceful haven after a weary journey. Inside, you are as likely to encounter someone taking a half-hour off to read the local paper or murmur a quiet prayer as a camera-strung tourist photographing the effigy of the local hero T E Lawrence that lies incongruously in the north aisle. Two features in particular lend themselves to its Saxon atmosphere. There are no pews, merely the open spaces of the floor and benches around the walls; the Saxon congregation would have stood for services, apart from the old and the infirm who were too weak to stand, and sat on the wall-benches (hence the expression 'he's going to the wall'). In the chancel and on the chancel arch, remains of the wall-painting lost at Deerhurst have recently been uncovered. Although they are 12th century rather than Saxon, they help the imagination cover the plaster with murals. The scene is of St Martin, the Roman soldier who gave his cloak to a naked beggar who turned out to be Christ. There indeed is the naked man, squatting, as Martin approaches on horseback with mounted attendants, and in a second scene Martin recognises Christ. Faded echoes of portraiture, these, telling a simple story to remind the congregation of the way to live, and, for a modern age that has forgotten the straightforwardness of teaching, such effectiveness of symbol requiring a printed notice to explain it all. The colours are now autumnal: russets, browns, yellows, pastel pinks and greens. But once there was a bold statement, bright colours and contrast where now there is only a pale memory of pigment.

Did the Normans stop here to give thanksgivings? In the brashness of conquest, probably not, and as they continued down the main North Street, they would have seen on either side fields and garden plots rather than houses, although still within the banks and crisscrossed with the lanes of the grid pattern. The concept of the town was still embryonic; the idea that an urban community could exist entirely by its produce or its services, and trade them with an outside world for food, had not yet fully developed. The fields and gardens helped supply the staples of life in times of peace; in time of war, they allowed livestock to be brought within the defensive perimeter. The arrangement could also support the gradual expansion of the population; fields could be sub-divided into smaller house-plots. In fact, much of the northern section of the town remained as gardens and orchards until very recently, as is testified by the modernity of the current housing there. The very northeast corner is still open, and a source of confusion to historians who could not fathom a raised rectangular area, looking like a parade ground, until someone pointed out that it was an 18th-century bowling-green.

There were, however, houses on North Street itself, set a little back from the actual road, and with their gardens behind; the boundaries of each plot were probably those to be seen today. In 1762 a fire destroyed much of Wareham, and the pretty little bow-fronts of the shops and the tea-rooms post-date this disaster[9]. In 1066 the houses were plain affairs, hovel-like to the modern eye[10]. With a structure of timber, in-filled with mud-and-wattle walls, there were no chimneys; the smoke was allowed to filter through the thatched roof, which at least had the advantage that it discouraged bugs among the rafters. Glass was very rare and very expensive, so windows were merely barred by wooden shutters against wind, rain, and thieves. The poorest, on the fringes of the built-up area, may have had a simple single or double-roomed house, and may have shared some of it with any livestock they kept within the walls of the town. The more established burgesses and merchants may have had more substantial houses, still with a central well for the smoke, but perhaps with a couple of first floor rooms over a ground floor area fronting the street for a workshop, storeroom, and business counter – the shutters would simply have been swung down horizontally to make the latter. Their gardens were more than a source of pleasure, they were also a necessity. They supplied vegetables – onions, leeks, beetroot, lettuce, pumpkins – and also herbs, used to season food in an age when spices were more valuable than gold, and the chief source of medicines. Flowers too were grown mainly for their medicinal properties, including roses, lilies, peonies, daffodils, and the purple iris; a plant like garlic combined the functions of a seasoner with a medicine (among other things, it was thought to be a good wormer, although judging from the remains of cess-pits, medieval man was riddled with internal parasites). Chickens could be kept in a garden, and also the ever important bees, for honey was the sole sweetener and the major ingredient of a favourite Saxon drink, mead.

Archaeological evidence has shown that the houses down North Street were probably set well back, and the Normans would have encountered some sort of industrial activity – a blacksmith, for example, alongside a tannery to wash and cure hides for leather goods, and another place where garden produce was useful, as tanning required quantities of the humble nettle in its process. If so, the Normans would have been assailed by a singularly unpleasant stench, for tanning was a smelly business. The further they rode down North Street, the closer they got to the hub of the town, centring on the crossing of the North/South and East/West Streets, and bordering on the dock area. Somewhere here the moneyers of the Domesday entry operated, for Wareham had its own mint. There were a series of these dotted around

---

9. Fortunately most of the population were at church, and no one died; after this, thatch was no longer used for roofing, although four thatched houses, spared by the fire, still survive.
10. Unfortunately, no house of this period survives in Britain, and any reconstruction must be speculation. The whole question is dealt with at greater length in the chapter on Newton Bromswold.

the country in important centres, an efficient and sophisticated system designed to maintain the value of the currency and royal control over it. The coins were called in every three years, and the dies for making them exchanged for a new set, for which the minters at Wareham each paid 1 silver mark and 20s. The coins were of silver, with the king's head on one side and the name of the moneyer on the other – some of the Wareham coins can still be seen in its small museum, scrubby little things with crude heads, but crucial to the economy of the day. The opportunities for fraud were no doubt there, but the penalties were severe – the minter's hand would be chopped off and hung above his workshop.

Here also worked the port reeve – 'port' being used to describe any authorised market, and not just a dock. It was he who ensured that ships planning to come up the tidal channel of the Frome stood off in the bay and obtained a licence before docking. A ship sailing up without such authorisation would be cause for the general alarm to be raised and shutters to be put up, in case it was a raider rather than a forgetful captain about to be fined for his transgression. Here, perhaps, was a merchant ship, unloading wine or other luxuries after a Channel crossing; the local fishermen discussing the state of the tide and the herring off Handfast Point; some clergyman from Somerset, looking for passage on his way to Italy. Across the causeway over the southern marshes trundled a cart, moving at a snail's pace behind its team of oxen, with a load of salt from one of the many salt-pans that dried out sea-water around Poole Harbour. Grain was being brought in, as there was little arable land immediately around the town; and loads of Purbeck marble for building, about to be transported by ship, although increasingly this traffic preferred the little coves of the quarrying areas to Wareham. An official from Shaftesbury Abbey or its nunnery might be there, supervising the cartage of salted fish. Merchants travelling through sold their goods wholesale, and left distribution and local sales to itinerant pedlars and sellers, and here they would haggle over the price, the merchant detailing the high cost of his long-distance overheads, the peddlar the impossibility of making a profit on anything so expensive, until a bargain was struck in time-honoured fashion. In amongst it all were Wareham's own officials, making sure that levies were paid as goods entered the town, and keeping its coffers full.

*　　*　　*

Down beside the crossing of the Frome was another church, the southern counterpart to St Martin's, and with the same functions; it was totally replaced by the present small Trinity church of Norman origin. Wareham had been a Christian centre even before Augustine's mission to England, and it is possible that Christian worship has been practised here continuously since Roman times. The Normans would have seen a number of other churches around the town – small chapels might be a better description – but they would have been making for St Mary's, down beside the docks, which towered over the thatched roofs and was one of the larger churches in England, with a nunnery alongside. The latter had been here since the 7th century, and was refounded by King Alfred's sister after the ravages of the Danes. The Normans would have wished to establish immediate relations with the clergy, and they would also have been curious about St Mary's royal connections.

St Mary's church, Wareham, beside the River Frome.

Somewhere in the church was buried at least one king of Wessex, but more recently it had been involved with a royal murder that had captured the imagination of the times. The young King Edward was staying in Wareham in 978 to hunt in the Purbeck Hills (yet another royal hunting area). On the evening of March 18th he was murdered at Corfe, to the south of Wareham, on the orders of his step-mother who, in true folk-tale style, was keen to see her own son, Aethelred (the Unready), on the throne. The churchmen at Wareham must either have been part of the conspiracy or else were cowed into submission: for although Edward was buried at St Mary's, the funeral was conducted without royal honours. The Queen and the church had not, however, taken into account the mystical qualities that the Purbeck Hills were supposed to attach to people who passed through them and to events that took place there. Miracles became associated with the body even before it had been carried to Wareham, and Edward the Martyr was quickly declared a saint. Two years later, in 980, his body was transported with great ceremony to Shaftesbury Abbey, which had realised the pilgrimage potential of the Martyr's spreading fame, and no doubt the income that would follow the pilgrims. They promptly built a shrine, one of the most popular until Thomas à Becket was murdered, and there the king's bones lay until Cromwell's soldiers scattered them to the four winds.

There is little of the great Saxon edifice in the fabric of the present church, and its nature has to be inferred from old prints. But one corner does house some remains of pre-Conquest Christianity. A 6th or 7th-century stone is set into the east wall with two others below it on the floor; all are inscribed with the native tongue of the times, early Welsh/Celtic rather than Old English. Nearby, a section of the floor is devoted to a whole mishmash of stone objects, neatly laid out. These include a tiny coffin lid, and an early oil-wick lamp, but pride of place goes to a huge coffin. In its design it feels Nordic: it is finished like some tub of a barge with the centre hollowed out in the shape of a body, complete with shoulders and head. You can well imagine it floating down the Frome, with an Arthurian sword rising out of it, and it is traditionally the coffin left behind when the monks of Shaftesbury whisked Edward away. It is much more likely to have contained Beorhtric, king of Wessex, buried here in 802. Its cumbersome tone is offset by another object, a beautiful fragment of a carving of Christ, looking like a stone model for a Blake painting and breathing that delicacy of feel which Saxon artists could so often create. It is now hidden away behind the bars of the chapel off the corner of the chancel, and is well worth ferreting out.

*   *   *

Such was the town of Wareham when the Normans took over, and it would be interesting to know whether they were met by curious townsfolk and a delegation of the chief men of the town, or whether they rode in to shuttered windows and suspicious eyes. There would have been good reason for suspicion, for something fairly drastic happened to Wareham in the following years. In 1066 there were 296 houses, with a population of between 1,200 and 1,500, mostly centered on the crossing of the main streets, but spreading out on their axes. By the time of the Domesday survey, there were only 146, a population reduction of some 40%; some houses were derelict, others had disappeared completely.

This destruction may have taken place on William the Conqueror's journey to Exeter in 1067, when he had put down a Devonshire rebellion. It could just as easily have been the result of the building of the Norman castle, an experience shared by a number of other towns in England. Understandably, William wanted castles built at strategic points, and the importance of this area is confirmed by the building of two royal castles, one at Wareham to control the sea traffic and the road trade routes, as well as to guard against any Danish raids, and the other at Corfe to oversee the quarry industries and conveniently placed for the royal hunting-grounds.

It obviously made sense to build the castle within the walls of a *burh*, but this involved not only the destruction of anything on the building site, but also of the area immediately adjacent to the castle. At Wareham it was placed in the southwest corner, with a large stone keep. Nothing is now left but mounds, though the curved lines of Trinity Lane and Pound Street (both of later date) probably follow the edges of the outer and inner baileys respectively. The responsibility for the castle building fell to the Sheriff of Dorset, Hugh, who was not surprisingly fairly unpopular. An addendum to the Domesday Book says of a pair of Dorset manors:

> 'When the Abbot acquired them, the two said manors were worth 100s more [than now] because they have [since] been plundered for [the benefit] of Hugh son of Grip.'

The houses themselves were owned neither by individuals nor by the community in the sense that we would recognise today. A large number belonged directly to the king, whose occupants owed taxes and services to him. Others belonged to the Church, or to chief landholders, and services and dues were paid to them. But the Church and the landholders in their turn had those properties from the king, and owed him their own taxes and obligations, in a pyramid structure with a king at the top, down through various layers of sub-letting and subservience, to the humblest workers. The town was sufficiently integrated into the hinterland for there to be little difference between town and country in this system.

Much of the town, together with St Mary's church, had been given by William to St Wandrille's, an ancient abbey on the Seine. Doubtless the occupants of these houses looked to St Mary's as their immediate superior, but others would look outside the town to different ecclesiastical establishments. Thus the Bishop of Salisbury maintained two burgesses in Wareham, probably to conduct his business there and to organise the import of goods through the port. A similar situation applied to the holdings of major landholders, and some of the houses can be seen as a kind of town adjunct to a country manor.

It was the king who granted (and took away) a town's status as a market and a mint, and the town as a whole did owe him certain collective duties. At Wareham, the most important of these was 'one night's revenue'. This was the amount required to maintain the king and his retinue for one night. As this could represent a large number of people expecting to be fed and housed royally, (it was the equivalent of a large sum, about £100 by the time of Domesday) Wareham probably shared the burden with other Dorset *burhs*. It was generally commuted to a money tax, but could still be demanded in kind if the king decided to hunt in the area; then it must have been a considerable, if exciting, disruption to the life of the town.

The question remains as to what happened to the population that was displaced by the castle. They may, of course, have died, either from military action *en route* to Exeter, or from the disease and famine that followed the poverty caused by the very high taxation immediately after the Conquest (in part, to pay for the castles). It has been suggested that the houses were still there, but by 1086 were too poor to pay tax and be noted in the Domesday survey. In the case of Wareham this seems unlikely: the Domesday Book specifically states that the houses were destroyed or derelict, and it is possible to sense a note of regret creeping into the entry, as if the assessors had ridden through the town slightly horrified at the waste.

In spite of the depredations, the town today retains more of its Saxon atmosphere than Norman, and it is ironic that while the banks still stand proud, the castle has to be conjured up in the mind's eye. Wareham gradually declined; as ships grew larger, the channel to the port got smaller, clogged up with silt and the rubbish of the town, its flow probably affected by new mills further upstream. Eventually ships found difficulty in sailing up the river, the products of the Purbeck Hills preferred other sea-routes, and there was not enough immediate hinterland to ensure Wareham's expansion as a market town. The inland manors wanted a closer outlet to the habour, and Poole gradually took over as the chief town of the area, although Wareham continued to have a fascinating and eventful life. The major Norman legacy is to be found in sections of St Mary's church, and in particular the 12th-century font, one of thirty lead fonts in Britain and the only one of hexagonal shape. It is moulded with figures of the Apostles, and stands on a base of Purbeck marble; the stone seems entirely appropriate, but somehow the lead seems a material alien to the spirit of this ancient town.

*   *   *

Today, as the sailing-boats and canoes clog up the little quay, tourist traffic looks despairingly for the signs to Corfe Castle, and the walks along the banks are surprisingly free of trippers, and still rural and open in feel with their thin growth of trees and hedge-shrubs, some qualities of the Saxon-Norman town cannot be recreated without recourse to a different mode of thought. A quick journey by car or train, and the whole of southern England is opened up; in 1066, although people did travel far more widely than is commonly appreciated, the worker carting goods, the merchant on foreign voyages, the clergyman on pilgrimage, the horizons of place were much more limited. The inhabitants of Wareham knew well only the immediate area; places further afield, even in Dorset, would have seemed like Alicante or Malaga to a modern British tourist. To be sure they had been there and seen it, but perhaps once a year, an experience equivalent to that of the annual holiday-maker.

Such limitations had their own rewards. With a small and static population, everyone in the town would have known everyone else at least by sight, rather like a rural community today. The major difference must have been at night. The darkness that engulfed the streets, with candles shuttered behind windows and perhaps only a watchman's lamp or a distant light on the hills, we can almost appreciate from the experience of a power-cut. But the silence we can never recreate. Even in the depths of the small hours there is always the distant rumble of a car, the chug of a generator, the muffled sounds of a late-night television. In Wareham in 1066 you would have heard the lapping of the tide, the cry of the nightbirds, and all the human sounds. A midnight domestic argument down the street would have been clearly audible; and as you certainly knew those concerned, and probably the cause of the row, doubtless you turned over and whispered to the wife 'They're at it again'. It must have bound people together; but it must have made the air of mystery hanging over the Purbeck Hills all the more tangible.

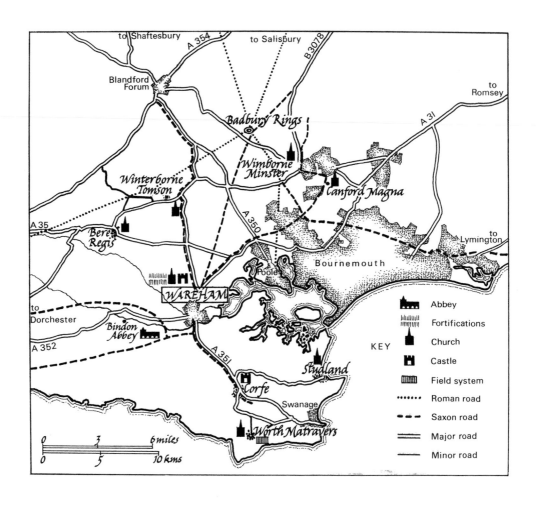

Traveller's Guide

Location of Wareham

SY 923877 (metric map 195; 1-inch map 178). From Poole (9 miles) and Bournemouth A351. From Dorchester (17 miles) A352. To Corfe (6 miles) and Swanage (10 miles) A351 south.

Parking: Apart from the limited and busy parking in the middle of the town, there is a useful car-park just outside the west bank.

Tourist Information: Housed in the public library near the South Bridge.

Other local Anglo-Saxon and Norman sites

Useful map: Ordnance Survey 1:25000 Outdoor Leisure Map no.15 **Purbeck**.

Bere Regis SY 847948: Large Norman church (12th century) and font.

Bindon Abbey (nr Wool) SY 853867: Remains of Cistercian abbey, unfortunately not open to the public.

Canford Magna SZ 031989: Church with Anglo-Saxon chancel (formerly the nave) with 2 porticus, and Norman tower.

Corfe SY 959824: Huge famous ruins of castle beside a pretty village. Virtually nothing of William's castle remains; current ruins of castle of Henry I and King John.

Studland SZ 036826: Classic early Norman church with squat unfinished tower. Ferry to Bournemouth from here.

Wimborne Minster SZ 014991: Major 12th-century church.

Winterborne Tomson SY 880970: Small Norman church; unusual survival of early single-space and apsed church with exposed timber framing, beside an interesting manor-house.

Worth Matravers SY 975775: Norman work in village church, including interesting tympanum. **SY 961755:** St Aldhelm's chapel: tiny building, 12th century, probably not a chapel but a watching or beacon house on headland. $1\frac{1}{2}$ mile walk south from village. Strip Lynchets: Terraced field-systems cut into hillsides to cope with expanding 12th-century population. In area to southeast of village and east of St Aldhelm's chapel.

Other sites similar to Wareham

Of the 30 or so burhs whose sites have been identified, most have either expanded beyond all recognition or shrunk into insignificant villages.

The closest parallel to Wareham is **Wallingford, Oxfordshire (SU 610890** metric map 174/5; 1-inch map 158), whose town defences, general layout, and interposed Norman castle are all quite easily traced.

The centre of **Winchester** still has some of its Saxon layout, while **Lincoln** and **Oxford** both have examples of castles that displaced a large number of houses and overlay the Saxon dwellings.

THE SAVERNAKE FOREST
AND GREAT BEDWYN

A Domesday Forest

Rex ten BEDVINDE. Rex. E. tenuit.
Nunq geldauit. nec hidata fuit.
Tra. e qt. XX. car una min.
In dnio fun XII. car. . . .

The King holds BEDWYN. King Edward held
it. It never paid tax, and was not assessed by hide.
There is land for 80 ploughs less one. In the
lordship there are 12 ploughs and 18 slaves.
There are 80 villagers, 60 cottagers, and 14
freemen with 67 ploughs. There are 8 mills
paying 100s. Two woodlands which are 2 leagues
long by 1 league wide. There are 200 acres of
woodland, and pasture 12 furlongs long by 6
furlongs wide. To this manor belong 25 burgesses. This town pays one night's revenue with all
the customary dues. In this manor in the reign of
King Edward there was a wood $\frac{1}{2}$ league long by 3
furlongs wide; it was in the King's lordship. Now
it is held by Henry of Ferrers.

If you were lucky enough to be equipped with the right kind of radar, and you focused
it on southern England early in the morning, an extraordinary sight would fill the
screen. From all over England, from the Midlands to the north, from as far away as
Devon to the west, from the fenlands of East Anglia, blobs would be seen converging
on London, like hundreds of spiders moving across a web to the centre. They are
flocks of sparrows, ranging into the capital for their daily activities, and in the evening
they all move in reverse, flying out to their roosts on the edge of the web.

Thus nature follows the habits of man, for snaking out from London, like some
tenacious ground-ivy, the tentacles of the road and railway system reach out into the
furthest corners of the land, until stopped short by the sea. Along these lines of
convergence the bulk of British journeys are made, and along their trajectories lies

the focus of the country. One of these arterial ways is the A4, the Old Bath Road, now superceded by the motorway to the north. But it still carries a full complement of traffic, much of it tourists meandering down west to Bath or Wells or the Somerset coast, and, as it enters Wiltshire, the charms of Marlborough, with its wide market street, its arcaded shops, and tea-rooms, seduce many into a break in their journey. But just above Marlborough, edged by the main road and probably unnoticed by the majority of travellers, sits Savernake Forest, older than the millenium, and on its southern edge the little town of Great Bedwyn, unsung and unheeded, whose name is unprepossessingly derived from the common name for the convolvulus, the bindweed.

London has been the centre of British events for so long now that it is difficult to envisage a time when the roads did not so comprehensively centre on the capital, when the loadstone of history and influence lay in other geographical areas. Undoubtedly London, with its position on the lowest reaches of the Thames, has been an important centre since time immemorial, but its pre-eminence was a product of the 11th century, and only conclusively confirmed in the 12th.

Until then, this corner of Wiltshire, almost in the middle of southern England, looked in different directions. It lies at the junction of two great swathes of chalk, the first to the south, forming the great Salisbury Plain and the landscape of Hampshire, the second a thin strip running from Marlborough diagonally northeast, through High Wycombe, Bury St. Edmunds, Thetford and to the sea at the north of the Wash. These are, for the most part, rolling upland plains, now characterised by great fields of wheat and barley, the occasional summit crowned by a crest of trees. Their undulations and valleys carry no water, for the rain runs through the chalk, the streams continue underground, and emerge only where the chalk is worn away to the clay, or another rock type intercedes. There is one such gash just to the south at Marlborough, where the River Kennet takes advantage, dividing the Marlborough Downs from Salisbury Plain; others let through the Thames or the Test.

This countryside, with its drained and easily cultivated soils, has always been attractive to man. In every part of upland Wiltshire can be found his earlier evidence, always shunning the marshes and the uncertainties of the river valleys: bumps of tumuli, scattered across the map like the Milky Way, the longer, more sinister mounds of longbarrows, the stone-circles of such famous places as Stonehenge, or the complex of Avebury and the huge, Christmas pudding-shaped Silbury Hill a few miles to the west of Marlborough. Along the tops lie hill-forts, gazing out over the flat lands of the Thames, guarding valley approaches, or vying for different sections of the plains. Along the uplands run the ridge-paths, the ancient trackways, that like so many of these early edifices have defied any later attempts at eradication.

The Romans had no need of such upland bias. They joined their centres with

70

straight military roads, and if Marlborough is a modern stopping point for travellers, Savernake Forest itself fulfilled the same function for the Romans. On the northern edge of the forest, across the River Kennet from the village of Mildenhall, a crook in the stream encloses a large field, the site of the Roman town of Cunetio[1]. Here the great road from Winchester to Cirencester, whose track can still be seen running across the forest, passed through, with villas dotted all along its way. Another road sped down to Old Sarum, and another came in from Bath; this must have been an important crossroads, whose axis was different from the modern roads[2].

When the Romans left, Savernake became a natural boundary for the kingdom later known as Wessex, and along the top of the Downs, from as far away as Bristol to the hill-fort at Chisbury in the Forest, the ditch called Wansdyke runs its course. Now at its best it is a high earthen mound with a deep ditch, with trees perched uneasily on its sides, curving like an earthworm through the fields. It was almost

The tree-covered earthwork of Wansdyke.

1. The field is known as 'the Black Field', like so many others that have turned out to be Roman sites. The Roman building materials blackened the soil.
2. The marvellous mosaic at the villa at Littlecote is just near the site of Cunetio.

certainly built in the 6th and 7th centuries as a boundary defence, demarcating the northern influence of Wessex, keeping Mercians and Angles away from Winchester and Sarum.

To the later Anglo-Saxons, the Roman remains (and probably Wansdyke itself) were objects of awe. In the popular imagination they were the work of giants[3]. To poets they illustrated the impermanence of earthly vanities. But the area retained Winchester as its capital, the seat of English kings, Alfred's city, the intellectual and administrative centre of Wessex[4]. Its importance continued into William's reign – it was here that much of the Domesday Book was put down on parchment. From the city roads radiated throughout the kingdom, to the southern ports such as Wareham, northeast to London, north to Oxford, west to Old Sarum.

If travelling from there up to Oxford, the area around Savernake must have been a natural stopping point, with Salisbury Plain out of the way, and the Marlborough Downs and the Thames valley to come. If people looked for somewhere to spend the night Marlborough was but a village; their choices were Pewsey to the west, and to the east Chisbury and Great Bedwyn. Now Chisbury is only a squatting of farm-buildings within the earthworks, and Great Bedwyn a smattering of houses which have forgotten that this was once a Wessex town, a minter of coins, a nameplace of substance. As the Anglo-Saxon poet of *The Wanderer* wrote:

'. . . Where are those men? Where is the hoard-sharer?
Where is the house of the feast? Where the hall's uproar?'

Part of the answer for the modern traveller is that the attention is focused on the ancient henge monuments, and the often fascinating evidence of Anglo-Saxon and Norman life is overlooked. The pre-Roman remains contribute little to the way man goes about his daily business; in contrast, many of the roads in the area, the villages, the siting of mills, the worship in churches, the copses of trees, even the very presence of Savernake Forest itself, are the direct heritage of Anglo-Norman life.

In this heritage there is something of an anomaly. In Bedwyn[5] there was the forerunner of modern town life with, at least in Saxon times, relative freedom for its inhabitants, and the start of the kind of commerce and organisations that would be recognisable today. In Savernake Forest, on the other hand, there existed a regimen

3. The name Wansdyke derives from 'Wotan's Dyke'. Whether it was so called because Wotan was worshipped here (as other place-names would suggest) in particular, or because later Anglo-Saxons thought that only a god with the powers of a Wotan could possibly have built such a structure is a matter of speculation.
4. One later king tried to revive the royal association of Winchester. Charles II commissioned a royal palace overlooking the city from the architect Wren, but only part of the fabric was started.
5. Little Bedwyn grew up after the time of the Domesday book, and therefore Great Bedwyn will here be referred to simply as 'Bedwyn'.

utterly alien to modern concepts, where the constraints on the movements of ordinary men were at their most acute. Yet the contrast was not mutually exclusive; on the contrary, the existence and function of a town such as Bedwyn was largely dependent on the Forest, and if its existence placed restrictions on the inhabitants of Bedwyn, it also brought benefits.

Both places belonged to the king; and both places owed their existence to the royal love of hunting already encountered at Kilpeck and Wareham. Indeed, a Norman king – and probably an Anglo-Saxon one – could have enjoyed the delights of the chase all the way up from Wareham to the Savernake, through Melchet, Clarendon, and Chute Forests, with William I's greatly enlarged New Forest just north of Bournemouth. Where the king travelled, a hunting retinue would travel with him; and, just as at Wareham, places were needed for overnight stays. These stays in their turn would attract vendors and traders, who would then naturally use the place on other occasions; and in this manner somewhere like Bedwyn could turn into a small market town and, to turn the wheel full circle, be granted royal recognition by the granting of such rights as the minting of coins.

By Norman times the lands under Forest Laws were an inescapable part of life; the forests themselves twined through the country like a common theme. Savernake Forest still survives as forest today, as do the New Forest and areas such as the Forest of Dean, and as such provides an example that in 1086 would be repeated from Land's End to the North Sea.

* * *

Hunting had, of course, long ceased to be an occupational necessity for the gathering of food; it had turned into a pastime of pleasure that also filled tables with luxurious meats. In the Welsh *Mabinogion* the excitement of the chase – here for a great boar – is already a special act, reserved for nobility and mingled with mythology and mysticism; and similar hunts, if not imbued with such metaphysical significance, must have been commonplace over Britain throughout the period leading up to the Conquest. According to William of Malmesbury, writing about Edward the Confessor:

> 'There was one earthly enjoyment in which he chiefly delighted: hunting with fast hounds whose opening in the woods he used with pleasure to encourage, and again the pouncing of birds, whose nature it is to prey on their kindred species.'

The Dane, King Cnut, shared this passion, and the Norman kings, from the Conqueror onwards, turned what had been a royal hobby into a royal institution, with its own rules and laws[6].

Where patches of ancient British woodlands had survived, and had not been cleared for timber or for cultivation, such areas must have been similar to the present New Forest, with its coverings of oaks and beeches, its mighty trees, its cool glades, and undergrowth of plant and animal life. But to the medieval world the word forest meant something very different from this nostalgic conception. Savernake could contain areas or patches of woodland that were the resort of ancient trees – Bedwyn Common may be one, and Hen's Wood (meaning 'Old Wood') to the north of the A4 was probably another – but the word quite simply described the area of the royal hunting-ground. King William and his retinue had no desire to chase through continuous woodland; at best it would be difficult and unpleasurable, at worst dangerous, with the quarry darting off through undergrowth, hounds lost through the trees, and the constant problem of fast riding under low branches. Birds of prey could not be loosed in the dense woodland.

Instead, what was needed was a variety of country, with open land as well as woods. Where Savernake is now tree-covered, much would have been chalklands with shrub or grass, or cultivated areas such as the fields you still come across in the middle of the modern forest, dappled with the occasional wood or copse. The most prized quarry was the deer, hunted by dogs that brought the animal down and were then called off. In the Savernake the gentle-faced fallow deer was the main species, as it still is, although red deer and roe deer were hunted elsewhere[7]. For closer contact with a more personal and dangerous adversary there was the wild boar, but these were already scarce by the time of the Conquest. But deer need some woodland, both for food and for the privacy of mating, and therefore a mixed landscape was essential for the royal pleasure.

*   *   *

In an age when the chief meats were mutton or pork, and the ox was used as a draught animal, not bred for beef, venison was easily the richest meat available, besides being large enough to feed the numbers of people that would form the king's retinue. But the deer is a shy and retiring creature that does not take kindly to disturbance of its ranges, and if the king was to have good hunting it was essential that

6. The lands under forest law reached their fullest extent (about one third of the total land area of England), and the laws themselves were most harshly applied, during the reign of King John. The Forest Law was one of the chief grievances of the Magna Carta, and in later years the laws were relaxed, and areas disafforested, if very gradually.

7. There is some doubt about the status of the fallow deer. Fossil remains have been found in Britain, but it may have been re-introduced by the Normans themselves towards the end of the 11th century.

the hunting grounds should be maintained for the herds. In addition, the deer would have been a tempting target for villagers for whom meat was a rare pleasure, and there were a whole string of villages around the Savernake Forest, and its associated hunting-grounds in the area. The forest occupied the higher ground; the villages, in contrast to earlier settlements, those lower areas where water issued from lower chalk springs, along the River Kennet, or on the line of the Hungerford-Pewsey road, a natural contour later utilised by canal and railway builders. Cnut seems to have had harsh penalties for poaching; but during the reign of King William the rules and penalties were prescribed in much less uncertain fashion.

The first necessity was to keep down other animals that might be harmful to deer, and rights of warren (in other words, killing) were granted locally for the hunting of foxes, hares, cats, and sometimes badgers and squirrels[8]. The second necessity was to limit the depredations of man, and here William departed from the continuity of custom and law that is so evident elsewhere in the change from the Anglo-Saxon to the Norman regime. The laws of the forest, codified in later reigns, were at the whim and desire of the king, and not based on traditions developed over earlier times.

To deter poachers, there were stiff penalties for anyone who harmed game – blinding or castration. The villagers around Savernake would have found nothing surprising in such penalties, or indeed in the principle, as the game belonged to the king. But what they did resent were the measures introduced to maintain the habitat of the hunting-grounds. On a simple level, dogs had to have three claws removed on each of the front paws – not such a simple matter if you relied on your dog to catch the occasional small animal for the pot, or to herd sheep. On a major scale, whole villages could be destroyed to make way for the forest, as happened in the New Forest, if not in Savernake[9]. The forest could enclose villages or their agricultural holdings, and it must have come as a shock to villagers and landholders alike to hear that their home had suddenly changed its footing because the king had decided to extend his hunting areas. Now, if you found deer grazing across the sheep pastures and tried to do something about it, you could lose your eyes as a result.

The kind of areas that now became royal reserves were often those, like Bedwyn Common, that had been common land, important to the farming economy. Up went the people of Bedwyn to the copses and woods to collect firewood, and to cut down larger trees for timber beams and building materials. Into those same woods they would drive their pigs, the main source of salted meat for the winter, to root around in the undergrowth hunting out acorns and beech-nuts; land was much too valuable to graze them elsewhere. On the chalk upland commons sheep could roam – ideal country, incidentally, as the well-drained ground prevented the foot-rot that could

8. The Normans themselves introduced the rabbit for eating, so it was not at this stage a pest.
9. Perhaps 2,000 people were displaced to make way for the New Forest.

afflict sheep on lower meadows. The open fields of the villages themselves stretched up into the forest land. Now any grunting pig under the spreading oaks was an interloper; the chopping down of trees was tantamount to theft; and, unless rights of warren had been granted, the capture of any animal, from a hare to a pigeon, was poaching. These restrictions were even more vigorously applied around Midsummer's Day, the date of Fence Month, when nothing was allowed to disturb the does and the new-born fawns. At the best of times, you could be stopped and questioned in the forest; then there was little if any movement allowed. A later report, when records were kept, illustrates the farming restrictions: William Russell's 120 acres holding should have produced around 30s profit; instead it produced 2s, specifically because it was in the forest[10].

To make matters worse, anyone accused of violating the forest laws could expect to be locked up for some time before his case was heard. In William's reign he had to wait until the Shire Court met; in later reigns he waited until the Forest Court met, which might be a matter of a year rather than a couple of months. Imagine what might happen to a smallholder rash enough, perhaps driven by the hunger following a dreadful harvest of 1085 and the famine of 1086, to kill a deer. Perhaps under straw, or behind cloths, would lie the evidence; at the door would come the knock, probably on the information of an informer (what opportunities the system must have given for neighbours to settle old scores!). A search, possibly a piece of small antler or deer bone being whittled into a household utensil on the floor, and the wife and children would be wondering whether their breadwinner would eventually return emasculated or sightless. Wandering down a Savernake Forest path today, with the density of younger trees cutting off any modern sight or sound, and with the occasional expansion of the path into a glade centred on a great oak, startled, maybe, by the sudden alarm-cry of a jay, it is not difficult to transport yourself back, to conjure a sack on your back, to scour for illicit firewood, to watch and listen, sharp-eared and nervous, against discovery.

In practice, things were not as bad as they might seem, although it puts Robin Hood – if, indeed, he ever existed – into sharper perspective: his most heinous crime was quite simply living in the Royal Forest of Sherwood and taking the royal deer. But William, true to his Norman ideas, had as sharp an eye for a quick monetary buck as for a four-footed one. Indeed, he was often as content to commission or appoint others to do the hunting as to take part in the chase himself: venison was required by households other than the royal retinue, and its sale raised money. Not only could rights of warren be sold, but the actual rights of hunting itself, and regularly in the Norman period the Church or barons would be prepared to pay very large sums to

10. I am indebted for this information to *A History of Savernake Forest*, by the late Marquess of Ailesbury, private printing, 1962.

The very large Norman church at Great Bedwyn, situated on the site of an Anglo-Saxon minster.

77

have their land removed from the forest laws. Pannage (the grazing of swine), firewood and timber collection, as well as pasturing, continued to be necessary to villages in or against the forest, and the fines imposed for so doing became in themselves a kind of rent. But if such activities were therefore tolerated, at any moment an arbitrary tightening of the restrictions could be imposed, and it must have bred a degree of constant insecurity.

Savernake, like the other forests, did not come under the jurisdiction of the county sheriff or the local reeves; instead, the king made his own appointments of trusted men such as William FitzNorman of Kilpeck. At Savernake there seems to have been an Anglo-Saxon equivalent before the Conquest, one Aelfric[11], described by the Domesday Book as 'venator' – the huntsman. William appointed Richard Esturmy, who probably sailed with the Conquest forces, to oversee the Forest. He was given much of Aelfric's lands, described as 'Terra Serventium Regis' (the lands of the King's servant), and his descendants were to manage, control, or own the Forest for centuries to come. Esturmy must have had other officers, and there is a glimpse of one in Domesday: Wulfic, described elsewhere as the hunter, who was tenant landholder in the village of Shalbourne, as were his family, and who seems to have acquired his land after the Conquest. Esturmy himself probably lived at Burbage, where he had land just to the southwest of the Forest, though it is tempting to think that he might have taken residence in the village whose name is most redolent of those Anglo-Norman hunting days, and which was included in the Burbage entry: Durley, from the Old English 'deor-leah', the deer's wood. It was, indeed, the deer who came first in the forest.

On the edge of Savernake, almost surrounded by the forest, with the main mass to the west and smaller offshoots on other sides, lay Bedwyn. In later years, extensions to the forest enclosed it totally so that it became a kind of oasis inside the forest laws. Above it, on top of the hill, are the strong banks of Chisbury fort, almost certainly the *burh* of the Burghal Hidage, and probably the earlier centre of population until it became too small, and its situation too uncomfortable, for the expanding population. At that point Bedwyn came into its own, down in the valley, with the strong defences of Chisbury available only half a mile away should the need arise. Later generations did not forget the hill fort either, for in the farm that straddles the bank is the gaunt shell of St Martin's chapel, its interior now empty of all but broken masonry and the detritus of starlings, its windows blank frames to the sky, like the eye-sockets of a discarded skull.

Bedwyn thrived and, by the time of the Domesday Book, was a prosperous place with around 750 people living in the town and the immediate area, its 200 acres of meadow presumably strung along the water-fed valley floor, and no less than eight

11. In the Latin of the Domesday Book, Aluric.

mills, water-driven and taking advantage of the streams and springs that issued from the chalk. Nowadays the traveller would probably never realise the antiquity of the place, for any memories of former glories are locked up behind the somnambulant bricks and paving stones, and the only fissure of excitement in the sleepy tenor of the town is the extraordinary Museum of Sculpture, covered with statuary, a riotous cross between a monumental mason's yard and an eccentric antiquary's pipe-dream. But there are ground-hints for the observant eye; Anglo-Norman patterns that have determined the shape of the town. Any trace of the Saxon minster is well and truly sealed under Norman foundations, but the squat and domineering Norman church is huge, quite out of scale with the place, as if an architect had misread his plans by a factor of two. The layout of the streets – a short and broad main street leading up the hill, little side streets at right angles to one side, and a great long street following the valley and passing the church to the other – follow the medieval pattern. In the main street itself, at the junction with Church Street, there is a large triangle, its function obscured by the equally triangular traffic island in the middle, and the petrol-station to one side. There, on the very spot where the white lines instruct cars to stop and the blue arrows circumscribe their direction, the market would have been held, with its direct access from all directions.

Here the town reeve, responsible for the borough town and its market, might be seen hurrying across, possibly to make arrangements for the shire court, which met in borough towns. Here, too, might be seen a couple of the 25 burgesses listed in Domesday, stopping each other to discuss some local point of order, for it was they who were responsible for the customs of the town[12]. It was these elevated gentlemen who were probably the motivators behind another of Bedwyn's institutions, one which heralds modern ideas, and seems to belong to a different plane to the forest laws. There was at Bedwyn what one now might call a mutual benefit co-operative society, and which is historically the forerunner of the trade guilds and, ultimately, of trades unions. Such associations were formed in conjunction with the church, and therefore tolerated by kings and local magnates, and their main purpose was to provide funeral arrangements and, at Bedwyn, five masses of psalters to commemorate the dead man. But they also fulfilled an insurance role, paying benefits for such things as fire damage. In recognition of their association with the church, the Bedwyn guild had to pay the parish priest a young sheep – or two pence – on Rogation Days. Their methods of operation have something of the ring of a modern club, with a subscription on entry, a probationary period before one was accepted as a full member, an oath to be taken, rules and regulations and fines for breaking them. The guild would also have had a meeting place, fitted out with benches for the

12. The Domesday Book is often unclear on whether burgesses lived in the town of the entry, or, living elsewhere, were attached to it for tax purposes. Here it is safe to assume that they lived in Bedwyn.

members to discuss important matters, and no doubt unimportant ones, too, far removed from the niceties of burial arrangements.

*   *   *

By the time of Domesday Bedwyn had already passed its heyday, and a glaring omission on the local landscape only confirms the decline – there is no Norman castle, and no remains of one. Marlborough was expanding rapidly to become the main market town and place of royal visit; the castle was built there, Bedwyn's moneyer transferred to the new centre, and the local traders gradually deserted the triangle for the new market place.

But in the meantime, everything belonged to the king: the forest on the hills, the town itself, even the right to hold a market in the town. Imagine, then, the excitement, the preparations, the trepidation, when William decided to exercise his royal prerogative of one night's revenue, and stay there overnight, to enjoy a morning of hunting in Savernake! Richard Esturmy and his men would be transversing the forest, finding out where the best bucks were grazing, checking that none of the hounds were lame. Into the town would be hauled sides of venison, to add their distinctive aroma to the night air when roasted on the spit. In their wake would come the market men, hoping to take advantage of the occasion, the singers and jugglers and tellers of tales to entertain the royal party or the townspeople (and, through their songs, to pass on stories of what was happening elsewhere in Europe). The town reeve would be busy requisitioning places for the royal followers to stay the night, no doubt meeting with some resentment, and the hurried concealment of a prized chicken or other potential food. The burgesses would be bustling about, ensuring that there was nothing untoward in the town to catch the king's eye; and in the church the most prized treasures would be dusted off, and preparations for the services made. Then would come the shout from up the Hungerford road, that the royal party had been sighted, and was on its way.

And somewhere, locked up, a villager who had taken a doe would be fearful at the advent of the shire court, while up in the thicket of the woods the deer would shiver at the distant howl of a wolf, and the bindweed search out another plant around which to twine itself.

Traveller's Guide

Location of Great Bedwyn and the Savernake Forest

Great Bedwyn: SU278646 (metric map 185; 1-inch map 167).

Savernake Forest: lying between Marlborough and Great Bedwyn, to the south of the A4.

From Marlborough A4 east, signposted south through Savernake Forest to Great Bedwyn.

From Hungerford A4 west, turn left at Froxfield (3 miles), signposted to Great Bedwyn.

Chisbury SU 279660: 1 mile by road to the northeast of Great Bedwyn.

Forest Office: The Forest is run by the Forestry Commission. The Forest Office is located off the A346 1½ miles south of Marlborough. Unfortunately, as the ownership of the Forest is still in private hands, the Commission is not allowed to issue pamphlets or maps, but will provide verbal information.

Parking and Access: The Forest roads are open to the public, with numerous off-road parking spaces. There are a number of delightful walks throughout the Forest.

Camping: There is a camping site adjacent to the Forest Offices, above.

Useful map: Ordnance Survey 1:25,000 **SU26** covers the Forest and the areas immediately adjacent.

Other local Anglo-Saxon and Norman sites

Alton Barnes SU 107620: St Mary's church: Tiny two-cell parish church with blocked-up Saxon doorway and Saxon foundations.

Alton Priors SU 109621: All Saints' church: Large, bare, and haunting church with Anglo-Saxon origins, largely superceded by St Mary's, above. The unspoilt and interesting villages (300 acres of whose land was given to William the Conqueror's cook) have now merged.

Chisbury SU 279660: Iron Age hill fort, later *burh* fort of Burghal Hidage. Ruins of later Norman Chapel in the farmyard.

Mildenhall SU 209696: Church with Saxon tower windows, and Norman tower, chancel and nave features. On the opposite side of the river is the site of the Roman town of Cunetio.

Ramsbury SU 274715: Site of former Anglo-Saxon bishopric (909–1058). Current church later, but contains heavily sculpted 11th-century cross-shaft with serpent decorations, and two carved tombstones of a similar period with foliate decoration.

Wansdyke: Parallel with A4, about 3 miles south. The best sections for walking can be found between the A361 (north of Devizes) and the A345 (Marlborough to Pewsey). There is convenient access on the minor road between Fyfield (on the A4) and Alton Barnes (see above). Other sections of Wansdyke can be found to the south of Bristol and Bath.

Other sites similar to the Savarnake Forest

The nature of forestry, the landscape, and land management have changed so much since the Norman period that, although sites such as Sherwood Forest in Nottinghamshire are to be found in various parts of the country, it is difficult to reconstruct their Norman extent on a casual visit. Three sites that are, of course, still heavily forested are Windsor Great Park, the New Forest, and the Forest of Dean, all of which have their own particular histories and beauties.

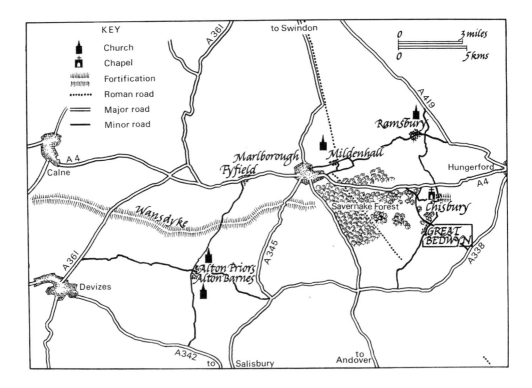

NEWTON BROMSWOLD

A Domesday village

De ipso epo ten Wills.II. hid dimid v min in NIWE-TONE. Tra.e.II.car. In dnio sunt . . .

From the same Bishop (of Coutances) William holds 2 hides, less ½ virgate, in NEWTON (BROMSWOLD). There is land there for 2 ploughs. In the lord's holding there are 2 ploughs; 8 villagers; 6 smallholders with 2 ploughs. There is woodland 2 furlongs long by 1 furlong wide. It was valued at 20s, now at 40s. Azor held it in the reign of King Edward.

There is still much to be learnt about village life in late Saxon and early Norman times, and in particular about the buildings that made up the village. The general picture may be known, but some of the detail must inevitably be a matter of informed guesswork.

In addition, villages and farming differed around the country much as they do today. In the higher lands of Devon or the West Country, for example, individual farmsteads were dotted around with field and farm boundaries that long pre-date the Normans, and which are often still in use. Newton Bromswold, however, illustrates a type of village and farming that was very much of its age, and which has now almost disappeared from our landscape.

Newton Bromswold has not yet been excavated; it offers great potential, and perhaps it will one day be tackled while so much remains under foot, untouched by the present day.

*　　*　　*

Perhaps the most personal thing that belongs to us is our name. Our names identify not only our present, but also our past, maybe an old family occupation, such as cooper, or a long distant relationship such as Johnson. Even our Christian names often echo a family tradition, handed on from generation to generation, or recall a grandparent, and are carried into the future in the naming of our children.

Yet few of us stop to ponder the names of the places in which we live or through which we pass. All over England, to a staggering degree, the names of the villages, the towns, the rivers and the counties have their origins far in the past, and most of them before the coming of the Normans. Here a syllable may have been taken away, there a vowel lengthened, a consonant mutated, a suffix added, a second name fused on. The language, too, has changed, and the commuter, naming his housing-estate home 'The Leigh' probably has no idea what it means, but the Anglo-Saxon who farmed the spot or the priest near Deerhurst would have understood instantly.

What a marvellous history book every road-map of England is, if only we know how to read it! Once in a while occur the earliest names, bestowed by the Celts before being driven west to Wales and Cornwall, and surviving subsequent invasion by Roman and Saxon and Norman: Leeds, Celtic *Loidus*, 'the district of the river', or London itself, its origin lost but linked with *londo-*, 'wild' or 'bold'. Roman camps and later towns are recorded in Latin *castra*, evolved into 'chester' or 'caster'. The early Saxons left their *ing*, 'the people of' and their *ham*, either 'village' or *hamm*, 'water-meadow', and often combined them with their own personal names. Later came *hamtun* 'home farm', and the Anglo-Saxons added their *leah* 'wood, grove, clearing', their *burg* and their *tun*, Scandanavians *by*, 'village', *thorpe* 'a secondary settlement' and *waite*, 'a clearing'. And these are merely the most obvious; other names recall gods, describe churches, reflect the purpose of the place, such as beacons, or record meeting-places. Some were even drawn from the characters of ancient sagas. Some, like Hampstead, tell us that the town, once a village, was originally a single farmstead. Others, like Oxford, recall that a village grew around an important functional location[1].

All too often Anglo-Saxon England is still imagined as a barbaric place, devoid of a sense of community or the permanence of dwelling that we would understand today: the myth of the 'Dark Ages'. Such a mass of place-names, passing across the continuity of our written history and still in use, however changed, tells us otherwise. England, when the Normans arrived, was carpeted with the basis of our modern human topography; some places were still farmsteads, but the majority were bundles of dwellings – the villages themselves. Today, even where hamlets are still hamlets, their origins are hidden from obvious view because we cannot actually see a Saxon building other than the very rare church; hardly a village in England contains a house earlier than the 15th century.

Sooner or later some beavering archaeologist will turn up a genuine Anglo-Saxon domestic building, long hidden under the encrustations of later modification and structure and initially unrecognisable, like Odda's Chapel at Deerhurst. For appearances can be deceptive: take, for example, the name Newton, as in Newton Bromswold, hiding in the corner of the map to the east of Northampton. It conjures

1. A dictionary of place-names, and a good eye for topography, can add a whole new dimension to a journey in Britain. For dictionaries, see bibliography.

up images of an 18th-century philanthropist, erecting a new village for his estate workers, or at the very least a medieval creation carved out of rough country when the population was expanding in the early 13th century. Not at all: Newton Bromswold was indeed a new town, a consciously created village, but of the 11th century, half a decade before William the Conqueror set foot on the shore.

NEWTON BROMSWOLD
after D. Hall, 1972

Showing village remains (modern houses and some modern boundaries omitted)

85

To call the place 'town' today would be laughable; even the word village would seem something of an exaggeration. The minor road from the northeast hits it, and rapidly makes a sharp z-turn at a point where a small scattering of houses, complete with an unlikely pub, define a lane off to the left. As the road continues it skirts what seems to be fields, interrupted by a smart village hall beside a church, and with a short row of council houses beyond. A little further, there is a house, Middle Farm on the map, and then the larger Manor Farm; and that is it. But that sharp kink in the road is significant, for it represents an old crossroads, and what was in 1086, and still is, the boundary between Northamptonshire and Bedfordshire; it lies just inside the eastern end of a rectangle. The road and its counterpart, half lane, half depression in the ground, mark out its long sides; a hedge just outside that scattering of houses and the drive to Manor Farm the short sides. Inside this rectangle, along with the church and the surviving houses, what looked like fields are a whole undulation of bumps and dips and hollows and the odd footpath or two: the only evidence that it was once built up as an organised and planned village. It is in places like this – deserted or shrunken villages – that one can perhaps best imagine the Saxon or Norman villager living out his life on the land. Here the attention is not distracted by all the later buildings and the inevitable alterations that disguise most English villages, however much they retain a Saxon ground-plan.

Half of the name has already given some clue to its foundation; the other half adds to the picture. The land runs northeast to southwest, comprising strips of Jurassic rocks with a covering of heavy boulder clay; Newton Bromswold itself is on a swathe of higher ground. There are still some isolated patches of wood, and in Saxon times it seems to have been a long stretch of woodland which they called *Bruneswald* – Brun's wood, commemorated in the name Leighton Bromswold, 'the *tun* where the leeks were grown in *Bruneswald*', some nine miles to the northeast[2]. Besides the then indigenous Saxons, the area is on the edge of that settled by Danes and Norsemen in the 9th and 10th centuries, and it may have been the pressure of such populations that persuaded a group (or their lord) to tackle the woodland, clear away previously uncultivated land, and construct a village. The new village was included in the Higham Ferrers Hundred, probably organised in the late 8th century, which followed the northeast to southwest orientation of the land south of a section of the River Nene[3]. By Domesday this was a thriving centre, about five miles to the north of Newton, and complete with its own market; in between the town and the village lay

2. The wood was not primeval; it was cultivated land in Roman times, and had gone to waste after their departure. Some older Ordnance Survey maps spell Newton Bromswold 'Newton Bromshold'; this error has now been corrected.
3. Higham Ferrers was larger than the normal 100 hides, and its designation as a 'Hundred-and-a-half' probably reflects the low density of population on land difficult to cultivate.

another prosperous settlement, Rushden, a concentrated village that boasted two manor houses, a church, and a mill[4]. In 1066 this area was a sub-division of the Hundred, the estate or Soke of Higham, owned by Gytha, the wife of Ralph, Earl of Hereford; by 1086 it was held by William Peverel, Sheriff of Nottinghamshire and Derbyshire, whose estate ran up against, but did not include, Newton Bromswold.

At the time of the Domesday survey, therefore, Newton can be imagined as a fairly new creation, at the most five generations old, and it is just possible that its oldest inhabitant would have been born before the village was created. Around and beyond were probably still areas of uncultivated land and woods; with its rectangular plan it was consciously laid-out, and did not simply spring up haphazard around a focal point. Walking across the jumble of mounds among the brambles, a pattern quickly emerges. Most obvious are the ditches or depressions running across the rectangle, some now accompanied by a scrawny hedge or a fence. These were paths, depressed into the ground by intention and by use, that divided the houseplots from each other, and which linked the two roads that ran either side of the village; indeed, a couple of the remaining houses still retain these ancient divisions as their boundaries. Some, if not all, of the spaces created were further divided so that one plot looked northwest, and its companion southeast, back to back. The other obvious features are the number of round depressions dotted among these plots; one still has the tell-tale darker patches of the grasses and reeds of wetter ground, and another, with a willow-tree bending over it and cattle munching beside it, gives the game away – they were ponds. On this higher ground, with heavier impervious clay, water must have been a rare commodity, and the little brooks on either side of the village were too far away to provide a secure supply. The very fact that so many of these ponds have now dried up suggests a possible cause of the decline of the village. Within the plots the more irregular mounds are the remains of the buildings themselves. Without excavation the actual date of these buildings is a matter for conjecture, but the plots and the lanes and the ponds have undoubtedly survived from the very earliest days of the village.

Down at one end was the manor farm, whose boundaries are still used by the present farm; a round mound in the field on the village side marks the site of the dove-cote, and until recently there was a very old stone building in the farm-yard that may have been part of the later medieval arrangements. Right up at the other end of the village is another mound, perhaps a windmill (not introduced to Britain until the 13th century), although the remains of a ditch that surrounds it could indicate an early and small motte guarding the crossroads. Those crossing roads are themselves much older than the village, part of the ancient system of ridgeways that kept

4. For much of the information on Newton I am indebted to David Hall, who, together with Ruth Harding, has comprehensively described Rushden and its history – see bibliography.

travellers clear of the more dangerous and marshier valleys, and the track to the southeast, gently winding up the slope, with the sloes and the elders ripening berries in the hedgerows, cannot have changed very much in appearance, apart from the impress of tractor tyres on its bed of hardened earth and clay. Yet not all is ancient or has disappeared in times long past: the plot on the northeastern corner of the rectangle has recently reverted to ploughed land, and there the cloying clay, sliced over by modern machinery, turns up a smattering of 13th-century pottery shards, and also a mass of familiar broken plates and broken bricks – the much more recent building has only lately been demolished.

What sort of lives did the villagers of Newton lead as the Normans took over? Domesday tells us something, but its bureaucrats reduced details to a cipher (as if the occupants had numbers rather than names) and blurred the distinctions of social status; as far as is possible, the rest must be gleaned elsewhere. However, the position in the small part of the village that lay in Bedfordshire – around the 'windmill' mound – was straightforward. Prior to 1066 it had been held by Alwin, whose lord was a major landholder, Burgred, and who could not dispose of the land without Burgred's permission. Such a situation never arose, for after the Conquest Burgred's lands were granted to one of William's chief ministers, Geoffrey of Mowbray, Bishop of the Normandy see of Coutances. He installed one of his stewards, William, in the holding of one virgate (normally a quarter of a hide, ostensibly 30 acres).

It was the Bishop who put down an uprising of Somerset and Dorset men in 1069, and he appears to have been a man who enjoyed his luxury. He once collared the English Bishop Wulfstan and asked him why he dressed in simple lambskin instead of the more luxurious furs to which he was entitled. On receiving an unsatisfactory reply, the Norman bishop then suggested to the English prelate that he should wear cats' skins. Back came the withering response: 'Believe me, we chant of the Lamb of God more often than we chant of his Cat.' Away from such exalted conversation, Geoffrey was also lord of the rest of Newton Bromswold, lying in Northamptonshire, which he had taken over from another major Anglo-Saxon landholder, Azor. This was also held by his steward William[5], and the value of the manorial holding was assessed at just under two hides (nominally 225 acres). When a general taxation was called so much was paid for each hide assessed, and after the Conquest the rate per hide was often harsh. There was land here to support two plough-teams, which the manor farm maintained. Besides this, there were 8 villeins, ordinary villagers whose wealth and status could vary widely and who are lumped together so frustratingly in the Domesday survey. They would owe certain duties to William the Steward and to

5. This assumes, as is more than likely, that the Williams of the two Domesday entries were one and the same person.

the manorial farm, but for much of the time they farmed on their own behalf, with, on average, around thirty acres of the common fields each. Lower than the villeins in status and wealth were the six smallholders (bordars) in the village, who probably held as little as five acres each, owned no oxen, and whose proportion of work for the manorial farm must have been much higher. Between them the villagers could muster up only two plough-teams, which suggests that none of them were especially prosperous, and the centre of the economy must have been the manor farm. The whole village, including the woodland two furlongs long by one furlong wide, had doubled in value since 1066, although this was probably more a reflection of military ravages in the area just before the Conquest, with a resultant depression in value, rather than any spectacular increase in productivity.

The ridge-and-furrow system of the medieval fields and Newton village on the skyline.

But these are merely the bare facts, the logistics of the village. Imagine instead that you are standing on the ridge above the Norman village early on an autumn morning. Around you, on the fingers of the higher land, up on the bump still known as Yelden Wold, the sun is rising on the turning leaves of the old Saxon woods. Down below you, the morning mist is lingering over the narrow stream, rather prosaically called the River Till, for 'till' simply means stream. On the far side of the stream, up a rise, is Newton Bromswold itself, its rectangle laid lengthways across your vision, and all around it the dew covers the open fields. Above the village the smoke of the house-hearths still lingers, confused by the warmth of the land and the cool morning air – not sitting on columns above chimneys, as in the classic picture of the lugubrious English Village, but in a general flat smog as the smoke seeps up through the thatch. There, on the right, the hollow way of the old track falling down before you is still in shadow as it traverses the village. Over there, on the left, the larger grouping of the manor farm and its well-defined boundary can be seen. There, in the middle, with smoke drifting around it, is the small tower of the church. And in between, as you start to walk down to look around, alerted by the crowing of the cockerels and the first bustle of the movement of animals and people, are the villagers' houses.

*   *   *

To get even the vaguest idea of what these houses were like, one now has to travel many miles from Newton Bromswold, to somewhere like the Welsh Folk Museum at St Fagan's in Cardiff. To this large park-like place have been brought, piece by piece, buildings of various ages from all over Wales, restored to the appearance and furnishings of their original date. Rather lost among the chapel and the tannery, hidden by tall and thick hedges, is a long, single-storied building, thatched and chimneyless, known as *Hendre'r-Ywydd Uchaf* – the upper farm in the township of the yew trees. To be sure, it belongs to a much later date than the Saxon-Norman houses of Newton – the end of the 1400s – but it is an anachronism, the end of a development whose salient features are not all that far away from 11th-century Newton.

The first thing that strikes you as you approach the house is its plainness; the simplicity of thatch and timber outline. Underneath that straightforward exterior, the method of construction is well suited to less developed carpentry techniques and to the limitations in the knowledge of load-bearing structures. At its heart are a series of upright beams (here six), curved over in pairs to meet in the middle of the top like the profile of a ship's prow set upright. Known as crucks, they were made out of the curving branches of, normally, an oak tree, and at Newton they were axed, chiselled, and then planed into shape with an adze. When these were hoisted and set upright, a series of long horizontal beams were put in place: the long ridge-pole where the points of the cruck met; others at the bottom of the crucks, to form a cill at ground level; and others, flown slightly out from the curve of the cruck to form the top of the walls and the eaves of the roof. The result is a kind of wooden framework in which each piece could be made beforehand and put up in a kind of prefabricated system. It is not known whether the Newton houses had a cruck-shape frame or a more simple box, but either way the result was much the same[6]. The very act of clearing the Bruneswald to create the village would have provided some of the timber for making

6. Whereas the post-holes may survive from 11th-century sites, the timbers do not, and the question of design is one of much academic debate.

the houses. As Byrhtferth of Ramsey noted in 1011:

'First you examine the site, and also hew the timber, and fit the cills well, and lay the beams, and fasten the rafters to the ridge-pole, and support it ... and afterwards you pleasantly adorn the house.'

Once this framework was built, the walls and the roof were added. As the roofing material was thatch, so much lighter even with a covering of snow than stone or slate or tiles, the framework took care of its weight and the walls did not have to carry any load. Short upright timbers between the cill and the top of the wall divided the wall into a series of spaces, which were filled in. First pointed staves were sprung in upright, slotting into grooves dug out of the main timbers. Then withies – flat pliable strips of branch from willows such as those growing by the Newton ponds – were woven horizontally in and out of the stakes. The wall was to all intents and purposes made; if ventilation were needed (in a barn, for example), the weave could be left uncovered. For a harder and more weatherproof house-wall, the weave was covered with a mixture of dung, clay, hair and other suitable material that set hard. In the *hendre* a layer of plaster was added to give a smooth finish, and painted white to give, against the blackened wood, the familiar and pleasing checker-board effect. At Newton, the walls were probably cruder, without such refinements, the wood left its natural colour. Indeed, the walls may have been even more primitive: either split planks dropped in vertically between the timber uprights, or the staves simply covered with a thick layer of mud without any wattle weave at all, though they would have been converted to the more efficient wattle and daub early in the medieval period.

A similar technique was used on the roof, its pitch a compromise between the steepness needed for snow to fall off and the flatness needed to give the least wind resistance. The wattle was made of thin rods, oak, sycamore, or other local timber, and onto this web was lain the thatch. The best materials were Norfolk reeds, almost universally used in modern thatch, but in medieval houses something more local had to be found. In spartan areas heather or turf might have to suffice, but at Newton there was a ready supply close to hand: the straw that was the by-product of the wheat and rye grown in the open fields. The straw was tied into bunches, and laid in layers up the roof, starting with the corners and the eaves. The bundles were fixed down with hazel stays, and the roof ridge needed the protection of a further layer of straw, which at the *hendre* is fixed with a little decorative criss-cross pattern.

The walls were, of course, pierced by the doors and windows – simple wooden frames, with wooden vertical bars in the windows, more to keep out unwanted people or animals than any attempt at weather protection. In particularly foul weather, shutters were put up on the inside of the windows, slipping into wooden grooves and the door was secured by a large wooden bar placed across the inside. From the outside the only sense of style is that created by the layout of timber work and windows. The lines are rough, never regular, for the carpenter's tools of the period could never produce an entirely straight line. The roof, too, has an air of softness, of pliability, for the edges of the thatch are rounded, and the simplicity is enhanced by the texture of the thatch and the uninterrupted roof-line. Open the door, and that air of simplicity is only compounded.

At this point, Byrhtferth of Ramsey would have adorned his house pleasantly, but he was talking of the houses of the rich and powerful, not those of such simple people as occupied the *hendre* or the dwellings of Newton Bromswold. Inside, all is barren; nothing relieves the bareness except that actual structure of timbers, punctuated by the wooden pegs that act as nails. Nothing that is except the wattle of the roof, discoloured by the tarry deposits of the fire, and forming a fascinating uneven pattern for anyone lying on a mattress and staring up, unable to sleep. Such decoration is a function of the building, not an adornment, for decoration is a product of spare time and spare wealth, and the villagers would have had little of either.

The *hendre* is divided across the width of the house into five sections (two for cattle, a service area, a central room, and a bed-chamber), but the Newton houses were not so elaborate, and consequently would have been shorter. The rudest may simply have had one rectangular room for both humans and animals, in which case a sleeping loft was needed – simple to construct, by placing poles across the roof space, lying on the horizontal timbers where wall met roof. But with the timber construction, the division of the building into two – one for humans, one for animals – was equally straightforward, as the wattle and daub could be used to fill the area between the two beams of the cruck, creating exactly the dividing walls that are found in the *hendre*. In a wealthier house this could be extended into a third area to separate sleeping space from living space, though in the grandest establishments, such as the Anglo-Saxon royal residences, the main building acted solely as the communal hall, and the royal sleeping quarters were in separate buildings.

In the poorest houses all the business of the household took place in the single main room. Its centrepiece was the hearth, the fire at the heart of the house, sited in the middle of the room. That at the *hendre* – a reconstruction based on early Welsh laws – illustrates what must have been the norm across medieval Britain. On the floor is set an area of pitched stone, about three feet by three feet, backed by a large vertical stone acting as a rear barrier. On the opposite side is a plain iron structure with two uprights – the firedog, across which the spit or cooking bowl was hung. There were many local variations, of which the ordinary tripod was the most simple, and more suited to the large cooking bowl of the predominantly vegetarian diet of the poor. The fire was kept burning constantly, and there would have been many curses and recriminations if it went out, for not only was relighting a fire with a flint spark on tinder a laborious job, but newly-lit wood sends out many more sparks than wood heaped on an already hot fire. With the smoke filtering out through the thatch, the risk of fire from sparks was ever-present.

Hendre'r Ywdd Uchaf at St Fagan's. People lived on the right, animals on the left, and the main central door served as a communal entrance. Note the shuttered windows and lack of a chimney.

A regular fire would have been needed anyway to keep the building warm and dry, and in winter it was essential. It also must have been a smoky business, as the underthatch at the *hendre* testified, but careful siting of the windows helped to create an updraught and clear any smoke that decided to take a different route around the room. The hearth-room at the *hendre* has two windows opposite each other, a practical response to varying wind directions. Around the hearth, the floors were of beaten earth, a mixture that varied from location to location. At Newton the earth was probably mixed with cow dung, chaff (to bind the clay together), lime if available, and ox-blood (a good congealant). The compound was laid on the floor and then beaten flat with a wooden block fixed to a long handle. On top went a covering, straw, rushes, or even bracken, an excellent animal bedding. In the human areas of the house the floor coverings were regularly swept out with all the rubbish that had collected, and changed. In the animal areas it was more carefully harvested, mixed as it was with all the dung and droppings, to be spread over the fields as manure and the only way of returning nutrients to the soil[7].

7. Straw from horse stables is, of course, still used as manure.

Such, then, is the kind of house that confronted you as you walked down the track on that autumn morning. If, on enquiring the way, you were invited in, the only piece of furniture that you would be likely to see was a large chest for storage. One such chest is to be found inside the *hendre*, but the otherwise bare interior does not tell the whole story, for the rooms need to be populated with the instruments of husbandry. To do so, you need to abandon our modern conceptions of possessions and imagine a different relationship with the objects around you. Everything had to have a function, an occupational place, and there was little room for objects of display or comfort in a poor house, and no place for anything that had to be quickly thrown away. Tools were handed down from generation to generation – as they still were on hill-farms until recently. All parts of the animals had to pressed into some sort of service: skins for leather and for shoes (sheep-hide made the best shields), guts for binding, hair to be twisted into string or rope, bladders for containers, bones for glue, combs, and other utensils, horns for cups, fat for tallow candles, the dung for manure. Wheat was broken down into corn for baking, seed for next year's crop, straw for thatching, chaff for bedding. A goose gave both meat and eggs, but also feathers and fat for ointments. Garden herbs were used to spice food, turned into home-grown medicines, and dyes for wool. Rosemary was hung over the door to keep away evil spirits (a most important function to the medieval mind) and, more practical, to discourage flies.

As you peer inside, over there behind the fire are the cooking utensils: a large cooking-pot, a ladle for stirring and pouring, a sieve for sifting meal, a bolter cloth for straining, and a mortar-and-pestle. Piled in the corner are wicker baskets and panniers for collecting and fetching produce, and a mousetrap to keep down the vermin that were inevitable with so much rodent food around. On the wall is a seed-bag for sowing, nets and snares for catching hares or poaching deer, and a gin-snare for wolves. Nearby are stacked the tools – a spade, a hoe and a hook for weeding, an axe, and a mattock (a kind of pick, with an adze on one side of the head and a chisel on the other). For the area devoted to animals there was a wooden rake for mucking-out, a brush-wood broom for sweeping, and the stall or manger for feeding.

A wheelbarrow was a handy, if more elaborate, piece of equipment for both the open fields and the garden. Gardens themselves were cultivated in the plot of land that surrounded each house, and were important enough for the Bishop of Coutances to claim '3 little gardens' in Isham, Northamptonshire, as the Domesday Book dutifully records. As well as useful flowers (also a source of dyes) and herbs, fruit, a few vegetables and bees were cultivated, and chickens scrabbled in and out of the beds, which were sometimes divided by low hedges of Butcher's Broom (*Rusticus aculeatus*) – a bushy evergreen with white flowers and red berries.

For most of the year animals and humans lived largely outside, the buildings being places of refuge only at night. But, as the autumn came to an end and the nights drew in, many of the farming activities ceased. The family got up with the dawn and went to bed with the night. If winter meant long nights in bed, that was at least the warmest place to be, a recharger of energies expended over the year. For those who did stay up, the atmosphere was fairly unpleasant – dim light, and the smoke from fire and candles exacerbated by windows now shuttered to keep out the cold.

Yet this was not a hibernating society; there were plenty of winter jobs to be done. Chief amongst these was the threshing of corn, separating the grain from the straw. These days machines make short work of the job, but until their advent it was a very slow and laborious task, the wheat being threshed by flails or double rods[8], and it could take all winter. The stacks of unthreshed corn-sheaves were stored on one side of the barn (presumably a communal building on the manor farm), and the stacks of threshed straw gradually piled up on the other side, though disproportionally, as bedding for the animals was periodically drawn off. Medieval yields were very low, and a large percentage of the grain itself was set aside for planting in the coming season.

Another winter job was the cutting of timber. Firewood was collected when needed, but wood for building or repair was at its best if the trees were felled in the period either side of Christmas. In addition, the branches were clear of foliage, and the ground of undergrowth. There was no need for it to be seasoned, except when needed for ships (when it would have been buried in mud washed by sea-water). Winter, too, was a season for hunting and trapping: beaver and otter on the rivers, wolf and fox in the rough country (all prized for the kind of furs Coutances suggested that Wulfstan might wear), and deer and hare for their skins and meat[9]. Inside the house it was the time for repair, for mending tools, for cobbling shoes, for patching clothes, as well as sorting the wool, dyeing, spinning and sewing, and preparing for the next farming season. And in some years winter was a time just for survival, for staying warm and fed, as in 1047:

> 'After Candlemas [February 2nd] came the severe winter with frost and snow and widespread storms; it was so severe that no living man could remember another like it, because of the mortality of both men and cattle; both birds and fish perished because of the hard frost and from hunger.'
>
> *Anglo-Saxon Chronicle*

But as soon as the frosts relented and the ground was no longer rock hard from the cold, it was time to start ploughing again.

8. In one tradition, known as 'Joseph and Mary'.
9. Beavers were not yet extinct in Britain, though it is not known whether they still survived in such areas as Northamptonshire.

Ploughing was a crucial activity for the farmers of Newton because the production of cereal crops, wheat, barley and rye, was the centre of the agricultural sytem, except in areas like the hill-country or the fens particularly suited to large flocks of sheep. The great open fields of Newton surrounded the village, and when the light is right the lines of the ridge-and-furrow can still be seen. The fields – better described as a block of land, for all the area is essentially one field – were divided into strips, the amount of land that could be ploughed in one day, on average about eight yards wide and 200 yards long. These strips were not patterns of dead straight lines; they ran up the gradients for better drainage, were inclined to twist a little because of the ploughing action, and mounds of earth (heads) would be thrown up where the plough turned at the end of the furrow. They also had to take advantage of changes of slope, and avoid natural obstacles, gullies, or the little stream to the north of the village. As a result, the strips formed groups of parallel furrows, running into other groups laid on a different alignment, and from the viewpoint of a buzzard floating lazily above, the whole open field must have looked like an irregular patchwork quilt. Each part of the patchwork was known as a furlong (a description of area, not the unit of length), and each furlong became known by its own individual name. There were no hedges within this pattern, merely the divisions of heads, drainage ditches, and the paths that gained access to the different parts of the field.

The strips were divided up among the various holders in the village, but an individual's strips were not grouped together in a block. Instead, they were allocated all over the field, a strip here, a strip there, so that the different uses to which the field was put, and which might require shared labour, could lie together. Thus one area contained strips belonging to various villagers (and the manor farm) which were all growing barley, another beans, and the system prevented one man's pea crop floating over to seed another man's wheat. With different crops in different stages of development dotted over the field, the patchwork effect must have been all the more marked. What is more, a rotation system was in operation – rather confusingly called the 'two-field system' (as that implies two fields, whereas all the cultivated land was one area) – in which only half the land available was actually in use in any one year. The other half was left fallow so that the soil could recover for use the following year.

In fact, by the time the frosts had fled and the ground was ready for tilling again, there was already a crop growing: corn (wheat or barley or both) sown at the end of the previous autumn, ready to push up at the first hint of spring. There were therefore two main corn crops each year, which eventually led Newton Bromswold to adopt a 'three-field' system: a third of the area for autumn sowing, a third for the spring sowing, a third fallow each year, though the date of change is uncertain. In the meantime, each spring the oxen-team trundled out dragging the plough, pushing the soil onto the ridge, laboriously turning at the heads. The sowing bags were dusted off to be filled with seed, and out into the furrow went the sowers – doubtless all the family – to scatter the seed on the soil, a scene not that far removed from the traditional biblical picture. There would go the wheat, there the barley, grown not just for breadmaking but for an equally welcome product, the malt for brewing ale. As the year went on, you might see rye at the top of the field, while the dark corner over there contains beans, and over there peas. You might also see some oats, and a more specialised crop such as flax for linen, or woad or saffron for dyes, all potential exports from the village and a source of monied return.

All these crops required attention throughout the growing season and many of the tasks, like ploughing, sowing, and harvesting, demanded a community effort, not only to ensure that the relevant strips were farmed simultaneously, but also because of the sheer physical labour involved. In spring the ploughing and sowing continued, and the autumn-sown corn, now pushing up above the ground, needed constant weeding to prevent it being choked by unwanted plants. As that crop started ripening, the spring-sown crop needed weeding, and birds looking for easy pickings had to be scared off. Soon the first corn was ready for harvesting, out would come the sickles, and the harvesters would move along the field cutting the stems close to the ground which others bundled into sheaves ready for carting to the threshing area[10]. Beans and peas had to be picked laboriously by hand, and while that was going on the spring-sown wheat had to be weeded before it, too, ripened, and harvesting occurred all over again.

While all this was taking place, slowly and methodically, at times upset by natural events – perhaps torrential rain turned a freshly ploughed field into a quagmire, or blight attacked a crop – the animals had to be husbanded. The most crucial and most valuable were the oxen, needed to draw ploughs and carts alike. Sheep were the most numerous animal in 11th-century Britain, but whereas most modern sheep are bred for fat lambs as well as wool, no lamb was eaten at Newton out of choice. The sheep supplied wool and were milked; by the time a sheep died and was eaten as mutton it was a pretty straggly affair. It was quite possible to keep a cycle of ewes in milk throughout the year and the cheese was a source of winter protein. Since sheep are hardy animals the villager would have tried to keep his flock intact throughout the winter, although numbers must have dwindled in exceptionally cold weather.

Those animals that were slaughtered and salted on the onset of winter were the surplus cattle for which there was no fodder, and above all pigs. Pigs were at the end of the animal scale, not allowed to feed on the cultivated land, and consequently they were lean and scrawny animals. There was no food available to maintain anything other than breeding stock over the winter, and pork was therefore the only meat

10. Newton had no mill. The corn had to be sent out for milling (there was a mill at Rushden) or ground by hand.

normally eaten by the poorer household. Beef and mutton represented animals that the farmer would much prefer to have alive, and hare or pigeon were an opportunist meal. At night the pigs were driven into a pigsty (if the plot had one), and the cattle into the animal house. The sheep were brought back from grazing every day to be milked. In winter the presence of the animals was welcome, as their body heat helped to keep out the cold, and if we would find the stench overwhelming, to the 11th-century villager it was familiar enough to go unnoticed.

The whole family was involved in looking after the animals, and because there was no concept of formal education the children were available to herd and shepherd. At times of ploughing and harrowing the oxen were employed in the fields, but ploughing traditionally stopped at three o'clock, partly to allow the beasts to graze. Grass for the cattle was not a problem in the summer months, as they grazed on the land lying fallow that year, but feed for winter was a crucial concern. Much of it came from the meadows, the land either side of the River Till; it was divided among the villagers in proportion to their holding in the fields and, with well-watered and often richer soil, was relied upon to produce a good crop of hay. Haymaking was another communal activity, one of those tasks in the farming calendar that has always been accompanied by a sense of satisfaction and a community spirit and was traditionally finished by August 1st. Then the cattle were driven in to feed on the aftermath and to fatten up, however marginally, for the lean months to come. Similarly the areas of the great field that had been harvested were thrown open to the animals, which also entailed the erection of hurdles to keep them from straying onto crops that were still growing. Sheep were moved up on to higher pastures of uncultivated land, to be looked after by that figure of the past, the shepherd boy, while his brothers and sisters urged on the pigs in the woods and the wastelands to feed on acorns and beech mast. Any goats that were kept lived off the rougher ground, and in winter the sheep had the open fields and the meadows, as well as higher pasture, to graze on.

In the village itself the women and the children had their own produce to look after: poultry to tend, bees to keep an eye on, cheese to be made, bread to be baked, the garden to plant. Sometime in the summer – usually early in July – the entire arable cultivation of the village came to a temporary halt to shear the sheep. These had first to be gathered, driven through the river, and ducked to wash out the accumulated dust and dirt. A thoroughly washed sheep needs nine or ten days for the fleece to dry properly; washing day had to be chosen with some care, as a sudden snap of cold or wet weather could play havoc with damp sheep. They then had to be gathered all over again for the actual shearing, and a pound created with hurdles to control them. Hand-shears were used, scissors-like cutters whose design did not substantially change from the Iron Age to the 18th century. After shearing the sheep were free to graze again, but for the women at home there was now the wool to sort, the surplus fleeces to be rolled and bundled for selling, and a whole cycle of dyeing and spinning and weaving to contemplate.

Standing in the village today, looking around at the remains of this forgotten way of life, it is not easy to cast yourself into the mind of the Newton villager. Three concepts in particular are alien to our modern civilisation. The first was the sense of the village itself; it was almost as important as that of the family, and for most of the time the buildings and the fields formed the boundaries of their lives, their work, and their aspirations. The manor might be a dominating influence, but it did not create the social cohesion of the village, only reinforced it, and many villages were divided between two manors, and therefore two masters. The second, which only reinforced that boundary, was the sense of community, created by the need for so many farming tasks to be shared in common; if that spirit failed, and those farming jobs were not done together, the farming itself would fail and the villagers starve. The third was the need for and use of money. The Newton farmer worked for himself, directly, in the sense that the products of his labour were consumed or utilised by himself and his

Newton Bromswold village, with the earthworks of a windmill mound in the foreground.

family – the intercession of money did not occur. Of course, money was needed to buy more specialised items such as shears or cooking-pots; surplus produce and specialised crops could provide an income, and the smallholders in particular could hire themselves out as labour to those with more land, or others (widows, for example) who did not have the man-power to cultivate what they held. Other members of the village had specialist skills in addition to their farming – the smith, for example, or the carpenter. But much of what the villager consumed he produced himself, in marked contrast to our own society when almost everything is bought, and money must pass hands.

The Newton villagers, however, did not just work for themselves; to a greater or lesser degree, according to their status, they worked for their lord, or his representative, William the Steward. For some this would mean direct service – they would work for so many hours a week, or days a month, on the manor holdings, and everyone would have put some work in on the manor farm at busy times such as harvesting or hay-mowing. For all it would mean some sort of rent, usually in kind – money at Michaelmas, barley and a couple of hens at Martinmas, a young sheep at Easter, loaves for the lord's swineherd, perhaps a share in looking after one of his staghounds; the arrangements would differ from area to area, and for the different villagers. Such villagers could not leave the village without permission, and they would have to ask the Steward's approval for a marriage.

Part of their lives was therefore circumscribed by the wishes of their lord; but the system still needed some kind of administration to decide disputes and conduct the business of the community. On the lowest level, there were the meetings (*moots*) of the villagers themselves. In these gatherings, the pressing farming questions were settled if they had not been ordained by the manor farm – when to start the ploughing, the arrangements for sheep-gathering, alterations to communal activities if the weather upset the farming timetable. Males over twelve were grouped into companies of ten (known as *tithing* in some areas, *frankpledge* in others), each man being answerable for the behaviour of the whole group, and one man being chosen as a leader or 'thingman'. Originally this concept had applied only to freemen, but gradually only men tied to villages or manors were in tithing – the freeman's own land, which could always be seized, was in itself insurance against his good behaviour. Twice a year there was a check to see that no one in the village was living outside one of these units, and the whole village was fined if someone was. Not only was it a check on the movement of the lower strata of society, but if the rights had been granted to the local lord by the king, it was a source of easy income. The tithing or village could also find itself penalised for other breaches of order, especially the chief scourge of the law, cattle-rustling. If the Newton villagers, mowing hay down by the river, noticed an unexpected file of cattle winding along the track to Knotting down on the rise to the south, and they failed to report it, they could end up being flogged when the cattle turned out to be stolen.

The next tier of administration to which the tithings were responsible was the Hundred itself. Although its composition might vary, it had its own officers – hundredsmen – who checked on trading and who would have ordered the flogging for Newton. At its centre was the Hundred court, which met every four weeks and was the main arena for settling disputes and administering justice. The court was usually held at a traditional open-air location – *moot-stows* – which might be a place of long-standing significance (a long-barrow, for example), and it only repaired to the local town in bad weather or the depths of winter. The *moot-stow* itself was a rectangular area, sometimes dug out expressly for the purpose, with the participants of the court ranged around the four sides, and the debating area in the centre; in the town this was copied by a rectangular arrangement of benches.

A whole varied representation of the people of the Hundred were required to make their way to the *moot-stow* every month, their journey conducted under a 'special peace' (in other words, any molestation would be punished by abnormally severe penalties). The king's reeve arrived, no doubt in some splendour; the major landowner turned up, or sent his bailiff, and the bishop or his representative would attend, for ecclesiastical cases were also heard at the Hundred court, and anyway so much important business was conducted there that the Church found it expedient to keep an eye on things. The lesser landowners, or their surrogates, found places in the rectangle, and finally representatives of the villages themselves, typically the parish priest and 'four good men'[11]. A panel of twelve (the distant ancestor of the modern jury of twelve) witnessed the proceedings.

Here in the Hundred court were heard what we would now call civil suits: an argument over the boundaries of a strip of meadow, a dispute over the ownership of an ox. It also heard criminal cases, and the procedure was simple and formal. The plaintiff – often under the auspices of the reeve, who had decided to bring some recalcitrant villager against whom many complaints had been laid to book – came before the court and swore on oath his dispute with the defendant, or the equivalent of criminal charges. The accused was then expected to come before the court and swear his innocence; if he failed to do so, the penalties were dire, leading eventually to him being outlawed. But assuming he did turn up, he swore an oath to his innocence, and was then given a period of time to produce witnesses to that innocence, the number required increasing with the severity of the charges. If these conditions were satisfied, and the witnesses duly appeared, he was deemed to have cleared himself.

If he failed to produce his witnesses, or if he had been caught red-handed in the crime, or if stolen property had been found in his house, then it was up to the accuser to establish the guilt of the defendant by producing *his* witnesses to the crime or dispute. Assuming these witnesses for the prosecution were produced, sentence was then pronounced: settlement in favour of the plaintiff in cases of dispute, a fine, a flogging, or mutilation for a criminal act according to its severity. The Church discouraged the death penalty, as death did not allow a person to repent of his crime, and it was normally reserved for crimes that especially threatened society: clear-cut treachery, burglary, and arson.

11. This duty was unpopular, as attendance at the Hundred court was a day lost on the farm. Eventually the villagers sent their own surrogates, those of less help on the farm.

There were methods of appeal against conviction. Some cases could eventually be referred to the Shire court, which met twice a year to deal with questions affecting the whole shire, and not just an individual Hundred. The defendant could also claim his now notorious right of ordeal, to demonstrate with divine support that his accuser and his accuser's witnesses were lying through their back teeth. He was a brave man – or his punishment was particularly severe – who would exercise his right, for it involved considerable pain and a high risk of failure. The actual ordeal was supervised by the church, and was accompanied by a fast and mass. The defendant had the choice of ordeal by fire or ordeal by water. In the former, he had to carry a red-hot iron for nine feet; in the ordeal by hot water he had to plunge his hand into boiling water and take out a stone. In either case, his hand was bound up, and if after three days the burns had not festered he was considered innocent. In the ordeal of cold water, he was thrown into water (after drinking Holy Water), and if he floated he was guilty. It says something of the attitude to the Divine that the ordeal for a clergyman was to swallow consecrated bread: if he was guilty, Divine intervention would ensure that he choked.

The Church might occasionally be involved in the rituals of the ordeal, but it exercised a more permanent influence on the lives of the inhabitants of Newton. Much of the present church building dates from the Tudor period; of the late Saxon church that must have stood on the site before the stone church nothing remains. This is hardly surprising, as the first church was almost certainly made of wood, its roof of thatch like every other Newton building. By some quirk of fate, part of a wooden Saxon church has survived in Britain, incorporated rather than replaced in later fabric. It gives some idea, however remote, of the kind of place that the Newton villagers would have worshipped in and decorated at harvest-time. To see it, you have to travel many miles to southwest Essex, just beyond the tentacles of outer London, to the village of Greensted.

The village itself recalls little of its early past, although it was a large manor in Domesday times, on a much grander scale than Newton. It was held by Hamo the Steward (whom we shall meet in the chapter on Colchester) and the village contained three free men, ten villagers, and 25 smallholders, not to mention slaves. Its woods were thought capable of supporting no less than 520 pigs, and among the animals were 40 goats. It was considerably older than Domesday, for there was a church in Greensted as early as the 7th century. The present Saxon nave was built about 845, and had a brief moment of glory in 1013. The body of St Edmund, a kind of British St Sebastian, who in 870 had refused to renounce his Christian faith in front of his Danish captors and was filled with arrows and beheaded as a result, was on its way to Bury St. Edmunds from London, where it had been in safe keeping. It rested here on the way, an object of great veneration.

Today only the Saxon walls remain in the immaculately kept church. But these are enough for the imagination to work on, upright logs split lengthways, and slotted between the ground cill and the wall-plate timber where the roof meets wall, so that from the outside the walls retain the roundness of the logs, while on the inside the surface is nearly flat. The timbers were tongue-and-grooved so that they fitted

The Saxon wooden nave of Greensted church showing the upright timbers. The porch, windows and roof are later additions.

tightly against each other, and the effect is rather like an American pioneer log-cabin with the logs vertical rather than horizontal. There were no windows, but eye-holes for anyone outside to peep in and observe the proceedings, and there is a niche cut out of the wood on the north side whose function is obscure, although it certainly was not the leper window of the popular myth. The pitch of the thatched roof was much the same as the pitch of the present roof, a Tudor creation which, with its carvings and dormer windows, is fascinating in its own right. Inside, the floor-space, as in other Saxon churches, was clear of pews. In the dark interior, lit by lamps that have left scorch-marks on the timber, with the crucifix above the entrance to the smaller sanctuary half-lit and flickering, the presence and the mystery of God must have felt very real to the worshippers. The church at Newton had something of the same atmosphere; its details – whether, for example, it had a tower – are lost under the masonry of ages with more solid structures.

The mysteries, the rites, and the regular worship at the village church all relieved the monotony of the farming life. But there were other recreations. Some can be deduced, such as the dice and other games carved from bones and found on Saxon village sites. Others, by their very nature, have left no trace. How did they celebrate such events as birthdays? There must have been music and song: the fiddle, the simple harp, reed-pipes are all folk instruments, along with various kinds of drum. The very fact that there are villages named after the figures of the sagas shows that the stories of the heroes and and the gods of Norse legend were old long before they were ever written down, and were not just the prerogative of the wealthy. So stories were told around the house-hearth, and no doubt many a mother frightened a wicked child with tales of Grendel.

Yet life was mostly hard work, the conditions difficult. The life expectancy was short, and infant mortality high, though it must always be remembered that if a person did survive the risks of disease and death early in life they could live to a ripe old age. To reach forty was to be old, and the numbers of those in their sixties must have been very small; consequently the very old were all the more venerated for the wisdom of their experience and their memories. But contrary to the almost universal misconception, the average height does not seem to have been much different from that of today – about 5′ 6″ for men[12]. A poor diet contributed to high mortality, and rheumatism and osteo-arthritis were an occupational hazard, along with a host of intestinal parasites. With predominantly vegetarian food, poor gums and teeth were another problem[13]. Hygiene was primitive, cess-pits dug outside as latrines, and at Newton the situation was made the more difficult by the lack of any stream actually running through the village. The large amount of standing water in the shape of the ponds was ideally suited to mosquitoes in a hot summer. The dividing line between survival and failure was very thin, and is best summed up by the *Anglo-Saxon Chronicle*, writing about those very years when the Domesday Book was collated and compiled:

> 'And this same year [1086] was very disastrous, and a very vexatious and anxious year throughout England, because of a pestilence among livestock; and corn and fruit were at a standstill. It is difficult for anyone to realise what great misfortune was caused by the weather: so violent was the thunder and lightning that many were killed. Things steadily went from bad to worse for everybody.
>
> Such a malady fell upon men [in 1087] that very nearly every other person was in the sorriest plight and down with the fever: it was so malignant that many died from the disease. Thereafter, in consequence of the great storms which came as we have already told, there came a great famine over all England, so that many hundreds died miserable deaths because of it. . . . So fever-stricken lay the

12. There is evidence to suggest that the Saxon profile was narrow, and that facial features broadened and flattened in the later medieval period, only to revert later on.
13. A rough wheat-based food wears down the teeth quicker than meat.

unhappy people in those days that they were never far from death's door, until the pangs of hunger finished them off.'

* * *

Such then was the life of the village of Newton if you had wandered down on that autumn morning. The Normans themselves did not leave much of an imprint on the village, but down the road they changed the landscape by installing a deer park, complete with boundary ditch and bank in a long rounded curve. They had to exchange some land with Newton farmers to do it, because it was near enough to encroach, and they also changed the county boundary in the process – you can still see the neat bulge on the map. Up the road in the next village of Yelden they built a motte-and-bailey castle complete with extensive outer ramparts, situating it on a corner of the Saxon village and covering some of the original house-plots. Today its fortifications are grass-covered but almost untouched, a textbook example of their military thinking. With the few houses and a cattery accompanying a village road grandly titled the High Street, it is a reminder of a busier and more populous time. Of the later history of Newton itself, and the reasons for its decline, little is known, but it must have still been thriving in the Tudor period for rebuilding work to be done on the church. Now, of course, it still survives as a tiny but busy community, the subject of school history projects for at least one of its younger inhabitants. Newton it may be on the map, and the Bromswold might have all but disappeared, but the village has its own intimate history, and today, if you walk down on an autumn morning and you see the combine harvesters crawling down the road to what were once the open fields, its own particular continuity.

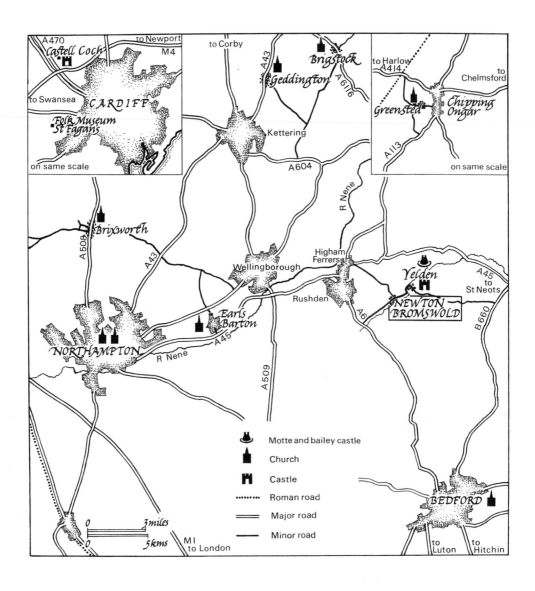

to Newport
A470
Castell Coch
M4
to Swansea
CARDIFF
Folk Museum
St Fagans
on same scale

to Corby
to Harlow
A414
to Chelmsford
Brigstock
A43
Geddington
A6116
Greensted
Chipping Ongar
A113
on same scale
Kettering
A604
R Nene
Brixworth
A508
A43
Wellingborough
Higham Ferrers
R Nene
Yelden
A45
to St Neots
NEWTON BROMSWOLD
B660
Rushden
A6
Earls Barton
A45
NORTHAMPTON
R Nene
A509

Motte and bailey castle
Church
Castle
········· Roman road
———— Major road
———— Minor road

BEDFORD

0   3 miles
0   5 kms
M1
to London
to Luton
to Hitchin

Traveller's Guide

Location of Newton Bromswold

SP 998658 (metric map 153; 1-inch map 134). A6 south from Rushden (4 miles via main road), turn left after $1\frac{3}{4}$ miles and follow minor road to Newton. A6 north from Bedford (13 miles), take same right-hand turn $11\frac{1}{4}$ miles after leaving Bedford.

Useful maps: 1:25,000 SP96 and TL06

National Museum of Wales, St Fagan's (St Fagan's Folk Museum) ST **114773:** (metric map 171; 1-inch map 154). From M4 take exit 33 and dual carriageway south. At next roundabout (4 miles) take first exit and turn immediately left (signposted to St Fagan's). Cross next roundabout, and turning for Museum is immediately after level-crossing on left.

Greensted TL 538030: (metric map 167; 1-inch map 161). From Chipping Ongar ($\frac{3}{4}$ mile) minor road west, sign-posted from town centre.

Other local Anglo-Saxon sites

Bedford TL 051501: St Peter de Merton's church: Anglo-Saxon central tower c1000 and other remains in the chancel.

Brigstock SP 946852: St Andrew's church: Fine Saxon lower tower and stair turret (late 10th century) and parts of nave and chancel.

Brixworth (see following chapter).

Earls Barton SP 852638: All Saints' church: magnificent Anglo-Saxon tower, the largest in Britain, heavily decorated with stripwork standing out in relief.

Geddington SP 895830: Church of St Mary Magdalene: Anglo-Saxon features showing developments in Saxon period followed by Norman work. Village famous for its Eleanor Cross, erected by Edward I.

Other local Norman sites

Many of the villages in the immediate vicinity of Newton Bromswold and the towns of Rushden and Higham Ferrers have echoes of late Anglo-Saxon or Norman times, and are rewarding to those who enjoy pottering about the countryside and are prepared to delve around for features that are now half-hidden or have half-disappeared: e.g. **Yelden (TL 014670)** remains of castle; **Swineshead (TL 057662)** moat site; **Riseley** moat sites (**TL 032626** and **TL 043634**) and a village that has moved across the stream; **Podington (SP 943628)** site of manor house; etc. The 1:25,000 maps are indispensable for such exploration.

Northampton SP 750603: St Peter's church: near site of the castle. Beautiful decorated Norman interior. **SP 756613:** St Sepulchre's church: circular plan nave of early 12th century based on Holy Sepulchre in Jerusalem.

Other Norman sites around St Fagan's

Cardiff ST 180767: Castle with Norman motte-and-keep. The Roman walls and major section of castle were rebuilt by William Burges in the late 19th century, the latter as an extraordinary fantasy.
ST 156781: Llandaff Cathedral: rebuilt in the 19th century. The Norman west and south doorways and east chancel arch survive.
ST 131826: Castell Coch: ruins of Norman castle rebuilt with evocative exterior and exotic interior by William Burges in the 19th century.
Note also: **ST 156871: Caerphilly:** post-Norman castle.
Ewenny SS 912778: Lovely and complete Norman priory church of former Benedictine foundation.
Ogmore SS 882769: Ruins of castle with rectangular keep.

Other Anglo-Saxon and Norman sites around Greensted

Pleshey TL 665145: Remains of Norman castle, and enclosure around village that may have Anglo-Saxon origins.
Waltham TL 381007: Holy Cross Abbey: originally founded early 11th century. Refounded as Augustinian priory (later abbey) in 1177. Now a parish church incorporating imposing Norman nave with drum-piers, gallery and clerestory. Restored by William Burges (see above, Cardiff). The traditional burial site of King Harold.

BRIXWORTH

A Domesday church

Rex ten BRICLESWORDE. Ibi sunt.IX.hidae dimid.Tra.e.XXXV.car.In dnio sunt . . .

The King holds BRIXWORTH. There are 9½ hides. There is land for 35 ploughs. In the lordship are 2 (ploughs); 14 villagers with a priest; 15 smallholders who have 15 ploughs. There are 2 mills at 33s 4d and 8 acres of meadow. To this manor belonged 1 wood which paid 100s a year. It is now in the King's Forest. To this manor belongs HOLCOT ... The whole paid £30 in the reign of King Edward. Now £36.

In trying to imagine a Domesday meal, there is one staple modern item that has to be removed – the potato. Take it away, and you more easily appreciate the reliance on wheat-based products such as bread, the humble dumpling, and beans. In much the same way, if you want to understand the 11th-century view of the world and man's place in it, you have to remove any idea of understanding based on scientific analysis, or at least in the sense that we now define it. Do that, and the questions remain much the same, but the answers have to be founded on the spirit and based in faith, and you begin to appreciate the reliance on God.

To the Christian, an understanding of his place in the universe was provided by the teaching of the church; to non-Christians, by the teachings of their various faiths. Therefore, ordinary men and women needed an intermediary between themselves and God, and that intermediary was, of course, the Church. The actions of the Church worked in two directions. Looking one way, it channelled the pleas and the aspirations of the layman to God. Looking the other, it interpreted the world, its events, and the religious code for the layman. In terms of how it affected people's lives, that second function was the most important, and one that has largely disappeared from the lives of the majority in the developed world today. One simple fact demonstrates the dominance of that role. Apart from noblemen – and certainly not all of them – clergymen were the only members of society who could read and write, and thus have access to what knowledge of the world there was, and to the moral concepts of the time. The spiritual and social power that this ability gave the Church was immense. On a political level, it meant that the royal court employed clergymen as scribes, who took down King Alfred's dictation, or sorted out and transcribed the mass of information pouring into Winchester that was the Domesday Book.

To gauge the all-pervasive influence and the permanence of religion you need look no further than the great Norman cathedrals, abbeys, and the thousands of parish churches. But their survival throughout the English landscape masks an earlier network of Anglo-Saxon religious buildings that covered the land before the Conquest. The very fact that a number of Anglo-Saxon churches do survive is a testament to the continuity of the Church, and if they seem like small fry compared with the magnificent structures of contemporary Constantinople, or with the Norman cathedrals, the influence they wielded on western Christendom was, from time to time, out of all proportion to their modest and homely appearance. And it is always worth remembering that if you lived in a two-roomed thatched wooden house they seemed neither modest nor homely.

We have already caught a glimpse of some of these buildings within the walls of Wareham and beside the River Severn at Deerhurst. But perhaps the most splendid, the most noble, of all these pre-Conquest structures (at least within the area covered by Domesday), enhanced by the simplicity of its location and the modesty of its modern surroundings, is the church of All Saints' at Brixworth, north of Northampton. In fact, the Domesday Book ignores its presence as it was in the lands of the king, although there is a sideways note in the mention of a priest who was there to serve the villagers, no doubt, rather than representing the complement of the church itself.

The origins of the building reach back to some two or three hundred years after the departure of the Romans, and have been the subject of much academic debate since the 1840s when Thomas Rickman realised that here was a Saxon church[1]. When construction first started, probably in the middle of the 8th century, England was by no means entirely secure as a Christian area, and the Scandinavian invasions swung the country between paganism and Christianity. The 7th century had seen widespread changes in the English Church, and its consolidation into the basis of the ecclesiastical structure that the Normans inherited. The great debate had been between two different systems of religious activity, the Irish (Celtic) Church and the Church of Rome. The Irish Church was based on missionary work, on men genuinely motivated by zeal who went out from such monasteries as Iona or Lindisfarne to travel, preach the Gospel, convert the heathen, and baptise. Their

1. T. Rickman *An Attempt to Discriminate the Styles of Architecture in England*, 5th Edition, London, 1848.

110

work done, they moved on or returned to their monasteries. There was no network of smaller churches, nor did they try to set them up. For converting the heathen, the system was ideal; for retaining their faith, on the other hand, and developing the religious life of a settled community it lacked the local presence.

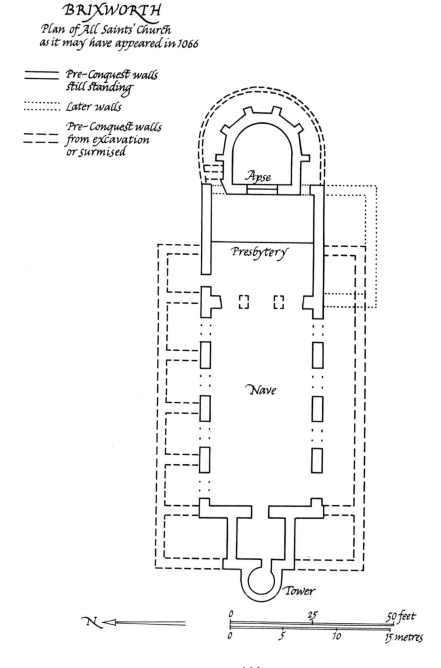

BRIXWORTH
Plan of All Saints' Church
as it may have appeared in 1066

Pre-Conquest walls still standing

Later walls

Pre-Conquest walls from excavation or surmised

Apse

Presbytery

Nave

Tower

N

0   25   50 feet
0   5   10   15 metres

By contrast, the Roman Church had a complex and well-established hierarchy: an understanding of the need for permanent organisation within a society, and the wealth and learning of Western Europe and its Mediterranean contacts to draw upon. Its idea of a bishop was a man of high position and standing as well as clerical learning, quite unlike the humble ascetic in the plain monasteries of the Irish persuasion. The more cumbersome structure was not nearly so suited to missionary work, but once the conversion of the British Isles had more or less taken place, it was widely recognised that it was time for the Roman system to take over. The matter was, to all intents, settled at the Synod of Whitby in 664. The idea of the modern Archbishoprics had already been laid down by Pope Gregory the Great in 634, dividing the country between York and London (for which was substituted Canterbury), and a Church with such a structure needed a network of establishments to carry out its work, not just the odd isolated monastery.

All Saints' at Brixworth seems to have been an early example of one of those establishments. It was sited strategically near the old Roman road of Watling Street (then, as now, one of Britain's major arteries), conveniently in the middle of the kingdom of Mercia. The question of its construction is rather like a good detective story, in which new clues (not all of them conclusive) surface with each fresh archaeological look at the church. The oldest clue seems to have been something of a red herring. Hugh Candidus, a monk of Peterborough, writing in the 12th century, stated that Brixworth had been founded as an offshoot of Peterborough Abbey (then called Medeshamstead), thus dating at least some of the church to around 670. However, he was writing some 600 years after the supposed event, and his evidence is suspect. As a recent survey has shown, the building materials were transported some considerable distance[2]. This would have been perfectly natural if the material was Barnac stone, as the Peterborough monks owned a quarry of such material; however, it is not, and it is highly unlikely that Peterborough monks would travel so far to purchase other materials.

A second contender is the great Bishop Wilfrid, who built stone churches in the north of England, notably Hexham, which bears some resemblance to Brixworth, and who spent eleven years as Bishop of Mercia. But there are stronger resemblances to churches in the south of England, and another candidate is Theodore of Tarsus who was Bishop of Canterbury from 668 to 690, and keen on extending his influence north. More likely than any of these is Aethelbald, King of Mercia from 716 to 757. From his origins as an exile in the Fens, he came to rule most of southern Britain, and there is a hint of contradiction in his personality. It was rumoured that he was a ravisher of nuns, and he was eventually murdered by his own retinue at

2. Diana Sutherland *Ecclesiastical petrology: the building stones of Brixworth church*, Geology Today. May-June 1985.

Seckington, near Tamworth; at the same time he knew the holy hermit of the Fens, St Guthlac, and St Boniface, one of the most celebrated churchmen of his time. Boniface was an extraordinary Englishman who spent most of his life working as a missionary in the Netherlands, and in Thuringia and Hesse (in modern Germany), ended up as a Papal Legate and Archbishop of Mainz, and was murdered at Dokkum in 754. He was also not above reproving the King of Mercia, and once banded together with other continental bishops of English origin to write to Aethelbald and suggest in no uncertain terms that he mend his ways. If Aethelbald did build the church, it may have been as a response to similar clerical criticism, or simply as an act of redemption for his sins. As will be seen, Boniface is more intimately connected with the church than a mere friend-by-proxy, and such a theory would give a date of around the middle of the 8th century, which seems to accord with the fabric. It would also explain why Brixworth is a royal church and manor, as detailed in the Domesday Book.

All Saints' church, Brixworth, showing the Anglo-Saxon apse on the north side.

At this point another clue works its way into the story. In 742 a major synod chaired by Archbishop Cuthbert was held at a place called Clofeshoh ('a high place cleft in two') whose location has never been conclusively identified. However, King Aethelbald attended the synod, so presumably it was in Mercia, and Boniface himself had a hand in the proceedings from a distance, writing to the Archbishop about the events and the discussions. From one side Brixworth does look like a high place with a cleft on the middle with the village on one hillock and the church on another. This is circumstantial evidence indeed, and the stuff of which legends are made, but it is certainly possible that Brixworth was the site of Clofeshoh and the synod. If so, the church was built in the years immediately preceding it, though, as Aethelbald had been reigning since 716, he had had plenty of time to undertake the work when he was not warring with neighbouring Wessex. Doubtless, it was already a hallowed site: perhaps a Celtic burial-ground or the site of a former wooden church, and this may have been the structure to which Hugh Candidus was referring.

Another branch of the story envelopes the actual fabric of the earlier part of the surviving church. Much of it is reused Roman material, but although a Roman villa has been excavated near the church, none of the material was filched from it. The most likely source seems to have been the ruins of Roman Leicester, 24 miles to the north, and confirmed as the see for Mercia in 737. There the Jewry Wall uses the same rock types in its masonry, quarried near the town. The Northampton Sand, which was used much more extensively in later periods of building at Brixworth, probably came from around Towcester where there were other Roman ruins. Roman ruins themselves were royal property in the 8th century, and so Aethelbald would have had a source of free building material. Carting stone was cheaper than quarrying and if he did build the church it would explain why the materials were brought relatively long distances to the site rather than procured locally. It might also explain the similarities between the arches of Brixworth church and the remains of the surviving Roman arch in Leicester's Jewry Wall. It is easy to imagine the mason, supervising the loading of the carts, going over to the Roman arches for a closer inspection, admiring their lines, calculating how the stones were laid and mentally appraising how the effect was achieved.

*　　*　　*

By the time of the Norman Conquest, a major crisis had been ridden out, one perhaps even more perilous to the medieval mind than other more concrete moments of disaster, such as the burning of the church by invading Scandinavians (a period when church-building virtually ceased right across the country, and much of it reverted to heathenism until the invaders were themselves converted). The origins

114

of this crisis were spiritual, even if the expected results were going to be material. As the millenium closed and the year 1000 approached, it was widely believed that the cataclysm would arrive, the world would come to an end, and the Day of Judgement would descend on all men on that auspicious date. With the advantage of hindsight, we now know that such fears were unrealised, as did Abbo of Fleury who wrote a book debunking them. Nevertheless the fear itself was real enough, and sufficiently strong that, after 1000, other dates were proposed for the end of the world, including 1033, which was supposedly 1000 years after the Crucifixion. The fact that harvests were bad and there was widespread famine during those decades seems to support such theories, as did the fall of Jerusalem in 1009–1010, but fortunately after 1033 there was a period of better harvests, a more optimistic outlook, and a general renewal of such things as church-building. The third stage of the tower and the stair-turret at Brixworth may belong to this period.

In 1066, slightly more of the church than we see today stood gaunt on the hill overlooking the valley below. As you wound up the path to the church, the countryside of Northamptonshire stretched out all around you, a different planet to the one we define today, for, as you perfectly well knew, somewhere far over the horizon the flat earth ended, and if you dared travel that far you would almost certainly fall off or be consumed by the fires that raged beneath. Up above, unseen, was the great glass firmament, encrusted with the stars, and the sun moving across the sky was encircling the earth, a flat plane of a world in a spherical universe. It too was full of portents, strange happenings that could be interpreted as signs from God, such as the Northern Lights, recorded in the *Anglo-Saxon Chronicle* for 979:

> 'This same year a cloud red as blood was seen, frequently with the appearance of fire and it usually appeared about midnight: it took the form of rays of light of various colours, and at the first streak of dawn it vanished.'

The appearance of Halley's comet in 1066, followed by the Conquest (it is depicted in the Bayeux tapestry) confirmed the power of such signs:

> 'At that time, throughout all England, a portent such as men had never seen before was seen in the heavens. Some declared that the star was a comet . . . it first appeared on [April 24th], and shone every night for a week.'

How the portent-mongers would have enjoyed the return of Halley's comet in 1986, the 900th anniversary of the compilation of the Domesday Book! Even the air around you was full of dangers – though probably not in a churchyard – for it was inhabited by usually invisible devils and demons waiting and eager to lead you into temptation or to jump on you. Many people (including senior churchmen) claimed to have seen them and their presence was universally accepted.

There was nothing so nebulous about the church in front of you. If you had been lucky enough to visit Italy, you might speculate on something of a Mediterranean hint to its lines. Up at the west end the tower presented a curious but satisfying contrast of geometry: a semi-circular turret (for the stairs) grafted on to the main square tower block. Small openings for light strode up the stair-turret, sometimes alternating with herring-bone work in the masonry, and down below porches swept out from either side of the main square tower-block. Behind the tower stretched the great nave, some 60 feet long, 38 feet wide, and two stories high. One-storied aisles abutted the nave on either side, joining on to the tower porches, their roofs sloping upwards to meet the sides of the nave itself, and making the whole thing 64 feet wide. Down at the east end of the church, the straight lines gave way to curves again, for here was an apse surrounded by an ambulatory, making the entire building 150 feet long.

Originally, the church housed a monastic establishment of the Benedictine order, who almost certainly left the church during the Scandinavian invasions of the late 9th and early 10th centuries, when the church suffered fire damage. Whether they reoccupied the church during the 10th century is unknown: there were no monks left there by 1066, but they may easily have returned, only to be dispossessed again when Earl Morcar swept through the area in 1065, and, in the words of the *Anglo-Saxon Chronicle:*

> 'The northerners [men of Northumberland and Yorkshire] did much damage around Northampton: not only did they slay men and burn houses and corn, but carried off all the livestock they could find, amounting to many thousands. They took many hundreds of captives, and carried them off north with them, so that the shire and other neighbouring shires were for many years the poorer.'

There must then have been outbuildings surrounding the church, for at one time or another the monks had to be fed and housed[3]. As you approached the church itself, the slow strains of singing filtered out into the churchyard; a service was in progress. On entering the church, the first impression was one of space, in contrast to Greensted. Where the aisles met the nave, a series of arches – those structures recalling the Jewry Wall in Leicester, and complete with their Roman bricks, set a little askew – led the eye to the central space of the nave, empty except for the congregation standing reverently for the service. The north aisle was divided to create side chapels complete with their own altars, and as you walked further into the church, you were faced by a triple arch towards the east end acting as a screen. This divided the nave from the presbytery which was unusually large so as to accommodate a monastic complement. There, priests and the monks, the former in their ceremonial finery, the latter perhaps in the black habits of the Benedictine order, conducted the service. This was a mystical act, celebrated in a language you almost

---

3. As yet, too little is known of these outbuildings to speculate on their extent or layout.

certainly did not understand – Latin – and which you, as a member of the congregation, witnessed, rather than participated in. Even Communion remained the preserve of those beyond that screen; the ordinary layman would receive the bread and wine perhaps only four times a year on the major feast days.

The south doorway of Brixworth church tower. The arch-head is made of reused Roman bricks with herringbone work above.

117

Another element added to the air of mystery: the use of music. The long, slow, declamatory effect of Gregorian chant has a kind of hypnotic air, but it could also be dramatic. The Anglo-Saxons built up different texts to tell liturgical stories or to celebrate mass, added the colour of a dash of two-part harmony, and sometimes children's voices could also be heard, for children were regularly left with monasteries for education, and often themselves became monks or priests. Instruments were also used. There was a celebrated 'iron' organ at Winchester (another Benedictine establishment), and elsewhere, if no such lavish organ was available, smaller portable organs or such instruments as hand-bells could always be put to good effect[4]. The singing, of course, all issued from the presbytery; Gregorian chant was a skilful business, and it could take ten years to train a cantor. However, if you were an 11th-century visitor you almost certainly came to say a prayer in the apse rather than hear the singing. For there, walking around the ambulatory, you would pause and gaze down a short dark tunnel into the crypt, which contained the relic of the saint you had come to revere and perhaps ask for some blessing, for a safe journey or for a sick relative.

*   *   *

The modern visitor is much more likely to hear a rousing hymn from the congregation than Gregorian chant, and will be lucky indeed if a monk is seen about the place, although some of the music that might have been sung has survived elsewhere in manuscripts[5]. Most of the church is still there, although the tower has had a spire plonked on the top, the nave walls have been decorated with battlements, and a later chapel has been added at the southeast corner. The ambulatory has all but disappeared. The chief difference is that the tower-porches and the aisles have been demolished, so that the arches once dividing aisle from nave have been converted into windows. The triple arch creating the presbytery has been replaced by a great single arch that gives a sense of enormity to the interior. One curiosity has escaped further rebuilding: a reused stone on the Saxon jamb of the main entrance doorway, on which is carved in low relief what is supposed to be an eagle, though nobody has properly identified it. Some suggest it may be Roman, others Assyrian. But what of the relic which was the object of such veneration in the 11th century? In that lies yet another clue as to the origin of the church.

At some point or other the church seems to have been dedicated to none other than St Boniface, that ex-patriot Archbishop of Mainz. His is not exactly a common

4. The Winchester organ was reputed to have had two manuals of twenty notes each, a total of 400 pipes, and require 70 men operating the bellows to get it into full song.
5. Some of this music has been recorded. For further details, see bibliography.

name for an English church dedication. Even more unusually, the relic that lay at the end of the short tunnel in the apse may have survived. For in 1809, a 14th-century reliquary (a container for a relic) which had been walled up (probably to avoid destruction in the Reformation) was discovered. It was made of stone in the shape of a miniature house, with pillars at the corners and a removable top with carvings representing a gabled roof. Inside was found a wooden box with a human throat bone and a piece of paper; the bone was a saint's relic, undoubtedly earlier than the stone reliquary, and presumably the relic that was the object of veneration in the apse. On the slip of paper was written the name of the saint to whom the bone had belonged, but in the best tradition of detective stories, it crumbled to pieces when the box was opened, before anyone had had a chance to read it. Did it say 'Boniface', and was the small bone taken from his murdered body on the Continent? We are unlikely ever to know, but the dedication of the church to St Boniface is strong circumstantial evidence. If, by some miraculous intervention of the saint, the reliquary could speak, it would no doubt tell us; but it now sits mute and inscrutable behind a cage of iron on the wall of the church, returned half-way to its walled-up state, minus paper but still with its bone.

The relic of St Boniface.

The font in Brixworth church.

The church at Brixworth, like that at Great Bedwyn, was a *minster*, a word derived from the Latin *monasterium*, and implying an actual monastical establishment in the former, but also a community of priests in the latter. Minsters were second in importance only to the cathedrals or the seats of bishops. There were 17 sees in England by 1066, and Brixworth was in the see of Dorchester, a huge area stretching through the eastern Midlands from the Thames to the Humber. Dorchester itself had taken over as the seat of episcopal authority for the whole region after Leicester had been lost to invading heathens (which was never restored to a bishopric). Being situated right at the southern end of this area, Dorchester was much more concerned with its interests in that southern end, so that outlying posts such as Brixworth were not in the limelight. The minsters were the central ecclesiastical establishments of their immediate areas; beneath them were first the ordinary churches with graveyards, which would be found in the villages or on manorial estates, and then field churches, rough buildings or chapels without a graveyard answering the needs of a new or outlying settlement. Newton Bromswold would probably have had some such building in its very earliest days. The system looked back to a time when there were virtually no village churches, and monks from Brixworth went out and preached at graveyards or beside crosses. By 1066 the parish network had built up, but Brixworth still expected the smaller churches to look to it, and every year at Whitsun the parish priests with representatives of their congregations processed to Brixworth in a kind of act of homage, taking their tithes and carrying back with them the consecrated oil needed for the coming year. It must have been an extraordinary sight; the solemn processions of the individual villages perking up as they climbed the hill, dusting themselves off after what sometimes would have been a long journey, the crowds milling around inside the church (for without any clocks or watches, no one could keep an accurate appointment or timetable), probably chattering away and exchanging gossip (it was a celebratory as well as a consecratory event), the monks dispensing the oil into containers tightly clutched by village priests, with the choir singing in the presbytery, and still others making their offering to the relic in the apse.

All these various churches needed some sort of income to support them. The cathedrals and minsters operated in exactly the same way as men of substance: they owned manors and estates, often on a very large scale, from which they received income and on which they also paid tax[6]. Often this land was increased by grants of estates by noblemen hoping to gain entrance to heaven through their generosity, such as Aethelric at Deerhurst. Some were exempted from taxes by charters (known as *bookland*), which were often hastily produced after the Conquest to prove exemption to the new rulers. Exempted or not, all were expected to fulfil the basic duties of defence and road and bridge building. In the case of Brixworth, a tier of

6. Over a quarter of English land, mostly in the south, was in the hands of the Church.

administration was redundant as its manor was directly owned by the king. The concept of a religious establishment taking a hand in defence was not seen as the contradiction it would be today, and there were plenty of fighting bishops to take a lead. Income could also come from fines, exemplified in a grant made by Edward the Confessor to a minster at Bromfield:

> 'I have granted to St Mary and my clerks at Bromfield . . . payments made as penalty for the breach of peace and for forcible entry into houses of other people and for committing ambush and . . . the right of doing justice on a thief taken within the estate in possession of stolen property, and that they be entitled to every fine within borough and without . . .'

Other income, especially on a parish level, came from levies imposed on the people themselves. Each working plough team paid a penny around Easter (plough-alms); at Whitsun there was a tithe of young animals; by All Saints' Day a tithe of arable and fruit harvest; a payment known as Peter's Pence was made on St Peter's Day; another known as *church-scot* at Martinmas; and three times a year, payment for lights for the church. In addition, there were fees for marriages, baptisms, and burials (*soul-scot*), and heavy penalties were imposed for non-payment. To whom exactly these payments should go was regularly a matter for contention. Theoretically Peter's Pence went to Rome and the Pope, though in practice in the late Anglo-Saxon period it was either not paid at all or reached other coffers. Originally, before the creation of village or parish churches, all payments went to the minster itself, and it still expected some of them, brought along at Whitsun with the vessels for the consecrated oil. Now village priests and churches had to be catered for, and, to further complicate matters, there was the question of the actual ownership of the lesser churches. Almost all of them had been built by the lord of the manor in which they lay, apart from a few that had been built by villagers themselves, and with such incomes coming in they were a source of profit. If some of the collected dues did go to the minster and for other purposes, much went to the lord of the manor, and smaller churches were let and bequeathed just like any other part of the estate, to the disapproval of some churchmen.

As to the disposal of the income that the church received, the situation was clearer, at least in the more pious establishments. Archbishop Wulfstan, that humble man who preferred the wool of the sheep to the luxury of fur, laid down that the income from tithes should be divided into three: one third for the repair of churches; one third for the housing and feeding of the servants of God, such as the monks at Brixworth; and one third for looking after the poor and slaves. His advice on the income from fines is also an indication of the kind of work in which the Church as a whole was engaged. It was to be spent on the provision of prayers, the welfare of clergymen, church repair, books, bells and church vestments, education, and the relief of the poor. In practice, the use to which the income from village churches was put must have depended on the character of the lord concerned, ranging from the conscientious, who would follow all of Wulfstan's suggestions through every hue, to the avaricious, who would appropriate the lot.

The position of parish or village priest was nothing like the regular appointment found today, especially as there was no concept of the parish as a unit of administration. The priest himself was almost invariably a freeman, but usually illiterate or semi-literate. He preached in English, and according to a later source, his duties were to expound at least four times a year the 14 articles of faith, the ten commandments, the precepts of charity, the seven works of mercy, the seven deadly sins 'and their progeny', the seven chief virtues, and the seven sacraments of grace. Of course, his activities were more than this. Wulfstan, who himself preferred to build churches rather than halls on his estates, saw the priest as the intermediary between villagers and the manorial lord, someone who would exhort the villagers to fulfil their duties to their lord, and exhort the lord to fulfil his responsibilities to the villagers. The priest's status was low; the monks, with their command of knowledge and the written word, must have seemed much more glamorous and authentic to humble people. To offset this, the priest wielded a certain amount of power and inside knowledge through the hearing of confessions. The priest was also likely to be poor, although the extent of his income depended on the character of his lord, and how much the lord was milking from the church. In some cases the priest actually rented the church (and therefore the dues due to it) off the lord, and expected to live off the profit; some of his income came from presiding at baptisms, marriages, and deaths. Many of the priests were married; some even kept concubines, in spite of attempts to impress upon them the need for celibacy. Some had a reputation for heavy drinking, and Byrhtferth of Ramsey, whom we last met advising on house-building, wrote a treatise on arithmetic aimed at priests in the hope, as he said, of getting them away from their dice to learn the science.

There were some 40 monasteries and ten nunneries in 1066. All of them followed Benedictine principles, and they existed entirely independently, without the mother church either in England or on the Continent. The image of monks toiling away at the simple tasks of the land, growing and gathering what they needed, is not entirely a truthful one, at least as far as these monastic establishments were concerned. They were more a loose-knit body of men who had decided to withdraw from the immediate secular world, and devote their lives to God. Ordinary tasks like farming could just as well be left to the villagers on the estates, and were. Bishops and other members of the clergy were closely involved with the administration of the day, even if they were not a direct part of it. There was one very good reason for entering a monastery (or a nunnery), and many men who had led active political and military careers did withdraw into a monastery later in life. For it was widely believed that, of the orders of men, only monks would go directly into heaven; and if you believed, as everyone did without question, in the reality of heaven and hell, a paradise to release you from earthly toils or the suffering of eternal pain and damnation, that was a pretty good reason for becoming a monk.

A less stern view of earth and heaven admitted a wider possibility of entry, but in a strict hierarchy: apostles, saints, hermits, monks, bishops, priests and laity, in that order. That ordinary people might believe that they could eventually go to heaven was due to the concept of purgatory, that limbo state between life and eventual placement in heaven or hell, and where repentance and atonement for sins on earth could be made. The concept seems to have been first propounded by Pope Gregory the Great in the 7th century, and it had an advantage for both minsters and priests. Relatives of the deceased wanted masses to be sung and prayers to be said for those who might be in purgatory, to increase their chances of reaching heaven, and they were willing to pay for such masses and prayers. Penitence could also, of course, be made on earth, and in a sense it was a religious parallel to the old Germanic secular ideas. Just as an offender had to satisfy the person he had offended by compensation, with the amount of compensation based on the type of offence and the status of the offender, so a sinner had to satisfy the offended God by the compensation of a penance, and there was a scale of sins with the appropriate penalties. The most superior penance of all was that of pilgrimage, undertaken by ordinary men and women as well as the noble and the wealthy. On the simplest level, pilgrimage could be to an English shrine, or to a relic – the bone fragment at Brixworth would be one such destination. More elaborate pilgrimages were made abroad to places with important relics such as St Sernin at Toulouse, St Denis in Paris (the church to which Deerhurst was granted) and, of course, Santiago de Compostela in northwest Spain.

The most prestigious European destination was Rome itself, and so many English people from all walks of life went there that there was a quarter of the city known as the School of the English, with its own hostelry, a fortified area with an English contingent of militia, and a church. King Alfred the Great himself petitioned the Pope for the exemption of this area from taxes, and his request was granted. There were hostelries along the route to Rome, catering not only for pilgrims but also for official travellers going backwards and forwards between Italy and the Channel. Some went on pilgrimage to Rome for the spiritual prestige, some because it was imposed on them as pennance, and others no doubt simply because they wanted to[7]. But it was a long, slow and hazardous journey. First of all there was the Channel to

---

7. One of the penalties for not paying Peter's Pence was to deliver it in person to Rome, but there is no evidence that this harsh punishment was ever imposed.

cross, with its dangers of shipwreck or capture by pirates. On the mainland there was the further possibility of robbery or attack by brigands – as the *Anglo-Saxon Chronicle* recorded for the year 1061:

'In this year bishop Ealdred went to Rome for his pallium [a woollen vestment conferred on archbishops as a symbol of office], and received it from Pope Nicholas. Earl Tostig [the brother of the future King Harold] and his wife also went to Rome: and the bishop and the earl suffered great hardship on their homeward journey.'

An Anglo-Saxon triple window in the west wall of the nave in Brixworth church. The blocked doorway once led to a gallery.

In fact, the bishop was left destitute, and had to turn back and request financial help from the Pope. But at least they did not suffer the fate of one 10th-century archbishop who was frozen to death while crossing the Alps. Other sufferers were the English women who were waylaid on the journey, and ended up as prostitutes in the towns on the route. The ultimate pilgrimage was to Jerusalem itself, an even more hazardous journey that might take years. Even after the fall of Jerusalem, Christians seem to have been tolerated in the Holy City (until the Crusades entirely changed the atmosphere), and another of Harold's brothers, Swein, undertook the pilgrimage. He probably did so as penance for sins that included the deceitful murder of King Cnut's nephew and the abduction of the abbess of Leominster, and he died on the way back at Constantinople. Many humbler people followed in his footsteps.

*　　*　　*

Pilgrimage represented just one facet of the intercourse between Continent and island. Not only did clergymen and emissaries from Rome travel to England, but English churchmen went to work abroad. Those who went to Germany or France are quite well documented, but of those who went out to Scandinavia, and who had a considerable influence in the conversion of those countries to Christianity, we know very little. They appear as shadowy figures across an inhospitable sea, preaching to the heathen of cold, northern lands whose great days of exploration and conquest were numbered. Another element of exchange was the revival of English art that accompanied the revival of monastic life after the ravages of the Scandinavian invasions, and reached its zenith in the 100 years before the Conquest. Although illuminated manuscripts came to Britain from the Continent, English illuminated manuscripts were greatly prized elsewhere, painted in an indigenous style known as the 'Winchester school' and whose main centres were Winchester and Canterbury. The style delighted in using leaf scrolls for initial letters, in a lively development of old designs of Celtic and Continental origin and in expressive figures with flowing drapes. It also specialised in line drawings in many colours. These manuscripts did not confine themselves to Latin religious subjects: there were lives of such figures as Alfred and Bede, as well as scientific treatises such as that by Byrhtferth, written in the vernacular.

It was one of the major tasks of monastic establishments like Brixworth to produce such works – and reproduce them by the only method available, copying – as well as to train younger monks in the skill. The vellum on which the manuscripts were painted was made of sheep hide (one hide being used for two pages in the largest books), bound in wooden boards covered with hide and decorated with gold, enamel, and precious stones. For inks and paints there were local sources, mineral and

125

vegetable dyes, carbon from soot for black, iron-gall (sulphate of iron mixed with oak-apple) for the characteristic brownish-black hue. The more exotic colours were extracted from materials that had to travel hundreds, sometimes thousands of miles along trade routes and caravan trails unknown to the monks of Brixworth except from fable. Lapis lazuli, giving that beautiful deep-blue colour, was mined only in Afghanistan, and, needless to say, these rarer colours were very expensive. The art of manuscript illumination was painstakingly laborious; but what satisfaction the monks must have had in choosing their sheep-hide for vellum, in mixing their colours, in inscribing a vine scroll here, in adding the craning neck of some animal there, in noting the characterful face of a worker in the fields and transcribing it to the head of a saint in the top right-hand corner.

Another aspect of this delight in colour and display was the spectacular use of ornamentation in church objects and decoration. The nave of Brixworth may have been empty but for people when you entered, but the walls would have been covered with colourful wall-paintings depicting scenes from the bible or from the lives of saints, like the faded example at St Martin's church in Wareham. Carvings, such as the stone eagle in the door-jamb, were decked out in bright colours, and on the walls were equally sumptuous ornaments, crosses burnished with gold or with silver, or figures of saints finished in enamel and precious stones, all the gifts of rich donors. The vessels and chalices were equally ornate, or made from the then rare glass[8]. English embroidery was famed, and the vestments of the officiating clergy were highly decorated with silks and materials interwoven with metals, matching the finery of the altar-cloths and tapestries. Alas, little of these riches have survived, although the Bayeux tapestry is a fine example of English needlework. The Normans were impressed by what they found, and promptly appropriated what they could for their own purposes, melting down where necessary and extracting jewels. Much of what survived them was then lost in the Reformation or in the puritan revolt against the ecclesiastical ornate. For a church like Brixworth it meant that the interior, however bare of furniture, was alive with colour and design, a cornucopia of imagery, the effect of which must have been something like a Greek Orthodox church today. The contrast with the ordinary village church, painted maybe, but much more crudely, and equipped with holy vessels, but nothing on the scale of the major ecclesiastical centres, would have been all the more marked.

*   *   *

The ecclesiastical system of which Brixworth was part changed dramatically with the advent of the Normans – as drastic a change as in any section of society, and

8. Some major churches had glass in their windows by this period.

comparable to the building of castles. The great drive of Norman cathedral, abbey, and parish church building has already been noted, but the tenor and the position of the Church also changed. Parish priests were perhaps the least affected, the senior hierarchy the most. Normans had been appointed to bishoprics before 1066 (one of them was appointed to the see of Dorchester, but was fired for being no good), and fairly soon after the Conquest Norman bishops took over the English sees, men who largely despised what they saw as the antiquated character of the English church with its use of the vernacular (particularly in parish churches) as well as Latin.

For the Continent had already seen reforms in the Church under the inspiration of the Abbey of Cluny, and these were brought to England by the Normans. The discipline of holy life was tightened (no more wives or concubines for priests), and new orders of monastic life replaced the easy-going, self-contained units, looking to mother-houses for control and guidance, and eventually populated by Cluniacs themselves, more rigorous Benedictines, and later, Carthusians, Augustinian canons and other smaller orders. More important, the relationship to the king and the state changed. William saw a potential threat in the English Church, a body essentially outside the control of the crown. Similarly, the Pope wanted the English Church to be more directly answerable to Rome and therefore gave William's invasion holy approval. The appointment of Norman bishops was one method that William employed; another was to separate ecclesiastical courts from lay courts so that bishops no longer made their way to the Hundred courts. The ecclesiastical courts were ultimately answerable to the king, and ecclesiastical estates were expected to fulfil their obligations to the king as much as any other estate. The Church was, in fact, brought firmly into the feudal system, and church manors were expected to provide knights and men-at-arms. William further strengthened his position by neatly sidestepping the Pope. Bishops could only leave England and papal legates enter with his permission; all papal letters were vetted by him; the Church could not take proceedings against any servant of the king without his approval; and no pope was to be recognised in England without his authority. He hammered home the point to the Pope in a letter by describing Lanfranc, the Archbishop of Canterbury, as his 'vassal'. The word exactly described the new position of the English Church.

Such changes signalled the end for such small Benedictine establishments as Brixworth, and there are no records of any monks there after 1066, if indeed they had reoccupied the church in the 10th century. Those English churchmen who could not come to terms with the new order moved north (where the monastic life had not been widely re-established after the Scandinavian invasions) or abroad; the rest had to accept the new realities. Brixworth was itself now far from any centre of importance and from the mainstream of political or ecclesiastical life. By 1086 not even the village itself was particularly large – 14 villagers and 15 smallholders, although the presence of two mills suggests that it served a wider hinterland, and it was not utilising all of its land. With potential for 35 ploughs, only 17 teams are recorded. It fades away from history, much to our advantage, for nobody had the wealth or the inclination to drastically rebuild such a large church until the Victorians sympathetically restored it. Consequently, we have, as we wind our way up the hill to the church, one of the great surviving structures of England before the Conquest, a place of pilgrimage to more than the relic of a throat-bone sitting in a reliquary on the wall. And, as if in memory of former ages, sheep still safely graze on the rich grass of its churchyard much as they did when Halley's comet put in its appearance at the beginning of the millenium.

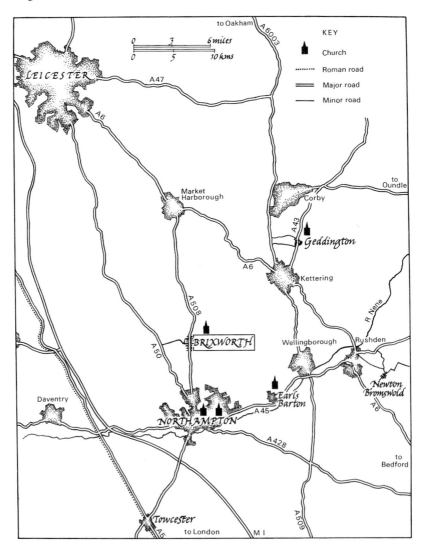

Traveller's Guide

Location of Brixworth

SP 747713 (metric map 141; 1-inch map 133). From Northampton (6 miles) A508 north. From Market Harborough (12 miles) A508 south. Motorway access: M1 exit 15, then A508 north to Northampton (3 miles). The Church is clearly signposted in the village of Brixworth.

Other local Anglo-Saxon sites

Earls Barton SP 852638: All Saints' church: magnificent Anglo-Saxon tower, the largest in Britain, heavily decorated with stripwork standing out in relief.

Geddington SP 895830: Church of St Mary Magdalene: Anglo-Saxon features showing developments in Saxon period followed by Norman work. Village famous for its Eleanor Cross, erected by Edward I.

Newton Bromswold [see previous chapter].

Other local Norman sites

Northampton SP 750603: St Peter's church: near site of castle. Beautiful decorated Norman interior. **SP 756613:** St Sepulchre's church: circular plan nave of early 12th century based on Holy Sepulchre in Jerusalem.

Similar sites elsewhere in England

A full list of the larger Anglo-Saxon churches is given at the end of the chapter on Deerhurst.

Colchester Castle.

COLCHESTER

A Domesday Castle

*Hundret de colecestra. In eade colecestra tenuit. God-
ric. I. lib ho tepr regis eaduuardi. IIII. mansiones. trae
. . .*

The Hundred of Colchester. In the same Colchester 1 free man, Godric, held 4 pieces of land
and a church in the reign of King Edward. . .

Just south of the town of Maldon, where the southern margins of East Anglia begin to
turn their attention to London, the long, straight road is flanked by a row of dowdy,
detached houses. The horizon is featureless, the landscape flat and blank; there is
not even anywhere to park, save a grubby verge or a bus-stop. Bisecting this row is
half a lane, half a road, attempting to keep disturbance to a minimum with a sign that
announces that cars may pass only with written permission.

As you stroll down the lane, the house gardens give way to corn-fields, pipits
twitter above, and to the north a chimney stack and a couple of spires on rising
ground mark Maldon town, a reminder of the derivation of its name: 'the hill with a
monument'. Further down the lane there is a crinkly old farm-house, Georgian in
feel, its windows askew, its roof undulating. It looks like one of those model houses
placed in a reconstruction of a battlefield in a museum, surrounded by little manikins
bearing stretchers and the legend 'King's Fourth Light Foot'.

Still the land releases nothing to the horizon to indicate the presence of the sea,
until suddenly a flock of gulls rises wheeling and screaming, and you realise that the
tall, braced pole rising from the ground ahead belongs not to the Electricity Board
but to an old fishing boat. A few steps further, and the road merges with the marshy
borders of the estuary of the Blackwater, and is quite literally gobbled up by the
waves. A pair of tall yellow poles surmounted by triangles (one for electricity, the
other for telephones) delineate the spot, with a matching pair across the water on the
edge of the small hilly island of Northey. If you wait long enough, and the tide turns
and the waters recede, the hump of the road – a tidal causeway – rises from the murky
depths to join island to land.

* * *

131

On August 10th 991 a band of East Saxons stood and watched almost exactly the same scene, for the landscape must have hardly changed, and even then there was a stone tidal causeway. This is one of the most evocative battle sites in Britain, where what would otherwise have been an entirely typical skirmish, rating only a mention in the *Anglo-Saxon Chronicle*, has been immortalised by an unknown poet, almost certainly a participant in the battle, and the author of the 325 surviving lines of the masterpiece of *The Battle of Maldon*[1].

The site of the Battle of Maldon, with Northey Island in the distance.

Holding a copy of the poem and gazing around, the battle unfolds for you. Over there, on the island, are a band of Vikings led by one Anlaf; on the far side of the island, with access to deeper water, are nestling the prows of his 93 ships, beached on the muddy edges. Already they have ravaged Folkestone, taken a look at Sandwich, overrun the land around Ipswich, and have now employed their favourite tactic of occupying an island as a safe base, either for wintering or else merely as a pause while deciding where to raid next. Up the road you have just walked came the East Saxons on horseback, led by a huge man in his late sixties, with swan-white hair, Byrhtnoth, Ealdorman of the East Saxons.

With him were his second-in-command, Offa, his hearth-companions (his warrior retine), and the general *fyrd* or levy. When they arrived, the tide was in and

1. The original manuscript was burnt in the fire at Sir Robert Cotton's library in 1731, but fortunately the librarian had already made a copy; by this date the beginning and the end of the poem were already missing.

the causeway unpassable. Byrhtnoth ordered his men to dismount, and sent the horses far to the rear of the position. The force prepared for hand-to-hand fighting, and one of Offa's men, to show his willingness for battle, set free his favourite hawk which was perching on his arm.

There was little that anyone could do while the tide was in, but from over on the island came a shout. The strong voice of one of the Vikings boomed across, suggesting that the Saxons came to terms, and give tribute in the form of rings and bracelets – not just for their intrinsic value, but as the symbol of the pledge of submission. There was no need for any bloodshed: the Vikings[2] would sail away, and consider the Saxons friends. Byrhtnoth scoffed at the idea, and his men jostled to the water's edge, just where the yellow poles stand, impatient for the tide to turn and the battle to begin. As the causeway began to appear, the local landowner Wulfstan (a kind of Saxon Horatius) took pride of place on the landward edge of the crossing, flanked by Aelfhere and Maccus:

> 'men of spirit
> who would not take flight from the ford's neck . . .'
> *(The Battle of Maldon, l. 80-81)*

Any Viking who tried to cross would be instantly struck down by these three, with spear or sword; the Vikings were unable to leave the island (they would not have been able to launch their ships with the tide out), and the tactical advantage seemed to lie with the Saxons.

But at this point the Vikings suggested that Byrhtnoth give them passage over the ford so that the two forces could face each other on flat ground and fight it out. This was within the rules of warfare of the day, appealed to Byrhtnoth's sense of honour (he seems to have been an exceptionally upright and pious character), and is an early instance of the British sense of fair play; but his acceptance was decidedly a tactical error. He drew up his men a little back from the shore, in the area of the field to the south of the present farm, and battle was joined. In fierce fighting, Byrhtnoth was killed. Under the Teutonic code of behaviour to which the Saxons subscribed, his men should have continued the fight, to avenge his death or to die in the attempt. But first of all Offa's kinsmen turned and fled, and one Godric actually leapt onto Byrhtnoth's horse and rode away, quickly followed by his brothers. But many of the Ealdorman's 'house-companions' stayed to fight it out to the bitter end, the 10th-century equivalent of defending the regiment's colours to the last man. In fierce hand-to-hand fighting they were killed, one by one. Olaf's Vikings held the field, but not before one Leofsunu declared the code of honour:

2. The Viking leader was almost certainly Olaf Tryggvason, later King of Norway; his 'Vikings' were probably mostly Norse – they sold much of their booty in France.

133

'I swear that from this spot not one foot's space of ground shall I give up. I shall go onwards, in the fight avenge my friend and lord.'

(l. 246-248)

In this code was embodied the ideal of the feudal relationship: the men are faithful and loyal to their lord, even after his death; Byrhtnoth is loyal and answerable to the king; and the king, at the top of the pyramid, came to be the symbol of those answerable to him – in other words, the nation. In this instance it was to no avail: the Vikings cut off Byrhtnoth's head and took it away with them, and shortly after the battle the first of many large payments to buy off the Scandinavians was handed over with the connivance of the Church. But the feudal system that the Normans developed was in many respects an extension of this pattern into fields other than military, and the spirit of the code infected British armies for centuries after a band of Saxons fell in a field beside the shores of the Blackwater[3].

The Battle of Maldon epitomises another feature that dominated Anglo-Saxon life: the threat of invasion from across the North Sea. Nor was this a new threat: the Romans themselves set up a series of forts along the eastern and southern coasts, and on the continental approaches to the Channel, and one of the reasons for their withdrawal from Britain was that the Empire could no longer sustain the complications and expense of the 'Saxon shore'. Those very Saxons whose descendants rode with Byrhtnoth had themselves migrated across the North Sea, and the 9th, 10th and 11th centuries saw wave after wave of raids, invasions and migrations from Scandinavia. For all the integration of peoples, the peaceful settlements, the trading networks – and these were considerable – there must have been long periods when the fear of attack and of destruction, especially on the eastern and southern coasts, must have constantly been in the back of people's minds.

The image of the bloodthirsty, horn-helmeted Viking, with bloodied battleaxe, raping and pillaging, is part of the inheritance of every British child, and through television and film has spread throughout the English-speaking world. Poetic licence has the Vikings disappear suddenly, as if all whisked off the seas at a stroke by some giant whirlpool, on the precise date of October 14th 1066, the Battle of Hastings. In reality, of course, the situation was very different. If, with historical hindsight, it can now be seen that, for a variety of geographical, climatic, social and political reasons, the Scandinavian countries became more introvert, and their influence waned, their contemporaries of the late 11th century had no such perspective. Indeed, the Normans themselves, some 150 years before the Conquest, had been a Viking band who had conquered and settled Normandy. The extraordinary influence of the

3. Byrhtnoth's bones, in Ely Cathedral, were dug up in 1769. The head was indeed missing, the collar-bone 'nearly cut through, as by a battle-axe or two-handed sword', and his height was estimated at 6' 9".

Normans throughout Europe is in part an extension of Viking energies and aspirations allied to a new social cohesion, exemplified in the sense of location implicit in the construction of castles and cathedrals.

Throughout William the Conqueror's reign, the threat from across the North Sea was very real. Cnut's control of England (he was also King of the Danes, the Norwegians, and some of the Swedes) was as recent as the second decade of the 11th century. Indeed, William's victory at Hastings was partly the result of tiredness on the part of the English troops. Harold, waiting for the expected invasion from across the Channel, was forced to march his army north at astonishing speed to deal with a totally different threat: the invasion by the greatest warrior of the day, Harald Hardrada, and his Scandinavian army. After their victory at Stamford Bridge the English army had to hurry south again to oppose the Normans, who had themselves landed[4].

Almost immediately after the Conquest, in 1069, the forces of King Harold's son joined with the 300 ships of the sons of the King of Denmark, ravaged Yorkshire, and wintered between the Ouse and the Trent before retreating. In 1070 the King of Denmark himself landed in the Humber and masterminded an uprising centred on Ely, and any wider danger was only averted by a great storm which scattered his ships, although a contingent did spend two days in London unopposed before returning to Denmark. An attempt at revolt in 1074 envisaged co-operation from the Danes, but the invasion fleet of 200 ships, unwilling to join battle with William's forces, preferred to land in Flanders. Perhaps the most serious threat occurred in 1085, when, in the words of the *Anglo-Saxon Chronicle*:

'In this year men reported and declared it to be true that Cnut, King of Denmark, was on his way hither, determined to conquer this country . . . When King William learnt of this – he was then residing in Normandy – he returned to England with a vast host of horse and foot from France and from Brittany which was greater than any that had ever come to this country . . . Men suffered great hardship during this same year, for the king gave orders for the coastal districts to be laid waste, so that if his enemies landed they would find nothing which could be quickly seized.'

In the event Cnut was murdered in Denmark, and his invasion fleet dispersed before ever setting out for England. Although the Normans were not to know it, this was the last concerted attempt at invasion from Scandinavia, and within another 50 years the spectre of the Viking prow had been largely forgotten.

*   *   *

4. Harald Hardrada had led an expedition to the Mediterranean, fighting in Sicily and Persia, and commanded the Varangian Guard in Byzantium (where he gouged out one Emperor's eyes), travelled up through Russia, where he married a Russian princess, and then ruled Norway. His story is vividly told in *King Harald's Saga*.

135

Faced with such a situation, William the Conqueror needed a base somewhere in southern East Anglia that would guard the northern flank of the approaches to the Thames and which would be a convenient strategic centre in the event of any internal uprising. He did not have to look far; some 16 miles up the coast from Maldon was a town that had, on and off, fulfilled such roles for over a thousand years before William ever set eyes on it: Colchester.

The town, even in Norman times, was associated with a multitude of legends and stories. The name of the town itself was drawn from the Celtic god of war, Camulos; and here King Cunobelin, better known since the days of Shakespeare as Cymbeline, ruled a large kingdom, the first objective of the Romans when they invaded in

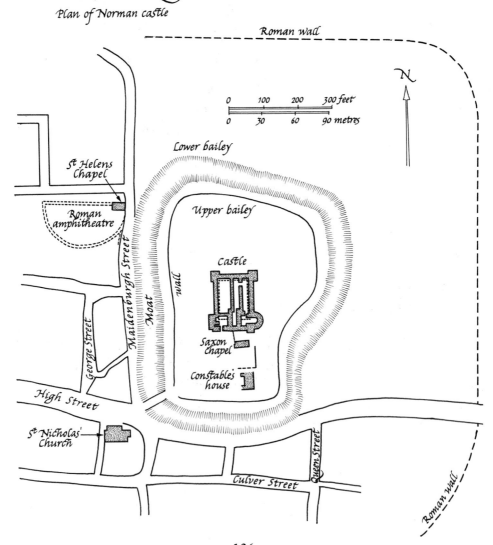

COLCHESTER
Plan of Norman castle

AD 43. The old British town was in the northwest area of the present city; the Romans moved their new establishment to a ridge to the southeast, and here, in AD 60, the most famous act of destruction in British history took place, when Queen Boudicca swept through, massacring everyone in the city, and burning the Roman buildings to the ground[5]. The Romans rebuilt, and early in the 2nd century surrounded, their ordered town with the strong fortification of a town wall.

When the Romans departed, the importance of Colchester declined. The great Roman buildings, including the Temple of Claudius which was the largest temple in Britain, gradually crumbled into ruin. Unlike some other Roman cities, it was, however, continuously occupied, the inhabitants building their ruder houses in among the Roman masonry, and, much more crucial, the Roman walls remained intact. The Danes knew a good strategic site when they saw one, and occupied Colchester, which was then the scene of another destruction:

'Then [921] . . . a great force gathered together in the autumn, from Kent, Surrey, and Essex, and from all parts from the nearest fortresses, and marched on Colchester and surrounded the fortress and attacked until they had captured it; they slew all the inhabitants, and seized everything inside, except the men who escaped over the wall.'

Anglo-Saxon Chronicle

The leader of this victory over the Danes was King Edward the Elder, who, faced with the same problem that now confronted William, had fortified first Maldon, and then Colchester, rebuilding the Roman walls and ushering in an era of prosperity and importance for the town.

By the time the Normans arrived, the population had grown to around 2,000, and if most of the buildings were undoubtedly in timber in an area where building stone is very scarce, the Anglo-Saxons had buried down deep into the collapsed rubble of Roman buildings to scavenge sturdy materials for their churches. The plan of the town did not follow the Roman grid throughout the area, and portions of Roman walls and ruins no doubt still poked their shadows above the ground[6]. Something very similar happens today, where in among the smattering of older buildings and the extensive modern reshaping, the occasional glimpse of Saxon structure can still be gleaned to recall the Conquest.

The road from London which the Normans would have used followed the wake of its Roman predecessor, and, as they approached the town, they would have been confronted with the reddish hue of the Roman east wall, no doubt with humbler buildings nestling up against it, and the drift of smoke hanging over the town beyond.

5. The layer of burning can still clearly be seen when excavations take place in the modern city.
6. In many places the Roman level is quite close to the present surface; in one area of excavation, the tar of the modern street was sticking to Roman mortar.

In the centre of the wall substantial remains of the east entrance, Balkerne Gate, still must have been standing, refortified by Edward the Elder. This had originally been a great Roman triumphal arch, but the Romans themselves extended its fortifications in the 2nd century. If the Normans had any illusions about making their own triumphant entry here, they were to be disappointed, for the road ignored it, skirted the southwest corner of the walls, ran a little way along their southern extent, and turned abruptly into Head Gate. The reason was quite straightforward: sometime around AD 330 the Romans had blocked up Balkerne Gate, and so it remained. The High Street, running east to west therefore stopped short of its logical conclusion on the east wall, and the Normans would have had to make a right-hand turn from Head Street to gain access.

The River Colne wound around the town, meandering from the west close past the north wall, and then curving round in a wide bend to the east before setting off for the sea to the south. Up the Colne would have come both trading and military ships, stopping either at Hythe (meaning 'landing place') to the southeast, or, if of shallow enough draught, rowing up against the north wall itself. The Saxon town had certainly extended outside the walls, for on the site of St John's Abbey stood a church, already extended and enlarged, and demolished to make way for the Abbey in 1095. Nearby, and still outside the walls, was St Botolph's, served by a small community of priests whose leader, Ainulf, led them to start the first house of Augustinian canons in England at the end of the 11th century, and to the foundation of the much grander priory that replaced the church in a typical Norman action. Another seven churches probably stood within the walls. These included the short-naved church of St Runwold's on the north side of the High Street; the important St Peter's which held land, slaves, a mill, and two houses; the recently built tower of Holy Trinity church; and St Helen's chapel, probably a wooden building rebuilt in stone and, in the process, incorporating a part of the Roman amphitheatre that lay under the foundations. In the northeast of the town, on a site that may have been used as a royal residence after the Saxon rebuilding of the town, was a chapel, originally of timber and wattle and daub, rebuilt in stone and decorated with wall-paintings, that was sited, by co-incidence or intention, close to the position of the.great Roman altar in the temple of Claudius.

*   *   *

The number of churches in 1086 was a reflection of the prosperity of the thriving town – an administrative and merchandising centre, a port with easy access to London and the Channel and to the hinterland of East Anglia. Most of its occupants were English rather than Norman, varying from the minor landholder with a house and a little land to burgesses of some wealth, such as Goda, who held 13 houses and 20 acres. The Domesday Book entry is a store-house of 11th-century names, most long deleted from our vocabulary. In among the Alrics and the Edwins lurk Godwin Weekfeet, Sprot, Shed-Butter, Tesco, and the three Gots – Got Chill, Got Hugh, and Got Fleet. There were, however, Normans living or holding property in Colchester, and the differences in social standing between conquerors and conquered are hinted at in the Domesday survey. Almost always the entries against Norman names carry the comment: 'they used to pay the King's customary due; now they do not pay': in other words, although still liable for general taxes, they were not liable for Colchester's customary fiscal obligations to the kind. This alone, besides their ancestry, must have set these holdings apart from those of the majority of the townspeople. The Norman landholders included some very important magnates. Hamo the Steward was the Sheriff of Kent, who had extensive holdings in Kent and Surrey as well as Essex, and a court in Colchester – in other words, a series of buildings built around a courtyard. Eudo FitzHubert, who was William's Steward, administered Colchester towards the end of William's reign, and performed similar services to the next two monarchs until his death in 1120. In Colchester he held five houses and 40 acres, and in Essex no less than 25 manors, as well as land elsewhere in eastern England and a castle in Préux in Normandy. He left his mark on the town by founding the Abbey of St John's and the leper hospital of St Mary Magdalen. Eustace, Count of Boulogne, held land in 12 counties. Otto the Goldsmith may have been responsible for making the dies that the moneyers collected every three years for stamping coins (his descendants certainly were) and he was to design and make William's ornate and jewel-covered tomb at Caen.

Of the occupations of the rest of the townspeople Domesday gives only the odd reference. Alongside the moneyers that operated the town's mint are to be found Wulfwin the summoner and such characters as Aelmer Milk and William Peche. Otherwise their occupations have to be inferred. At the lowest level were those that any community needed; smiths, bakers, millers, seamstresses, carpenters, potters, butchers. Other occupations were more specialised and, if not exclusively urban, tended to congregate in such centres as Colchester to where the raw materials were brought in larger quantities – the clothing trade, for example, with tanners, leather-workers, wool-workers, dyers and the small industries that supplied them with tools and with such items as buckles. Then there were specialist skills that were more specifically urban, such as jewellers, goldsmiths, weaponsmiths, or makers of luxury items for the Church or for richer homes. But many at Colchester were simply merchants; the lesser ones travelling from market-place to market-place around England, buying and selling possibly with a base in Colchester, and the more important merchants travelling abroad importing and exporting. Into the port of

Colchester came such things as spices, exotic dyes, chain-mail, glass, and wine. Out would go prized English products such as needlework. Wool, woollen products, and grain were both exported and imported. Some of the burgesses were agents for estates in the hinterland that needed to trade and import and export, and to support this commerce financiers were needed. The Church discouraged Christians acting as usurers, and so Jews, who were restricted from following other trades, became the main financiers, and there is some evidence to suggest that it was William who brought them to Britain to support his fiscal policy.

One of the corner towers of Colchester Castle.

140

A sign of the prosperity of Colchester was the classification of the town for fiscal purposes as a Hundred, normally reserved for a large agricultural area, equating it with a nominal 100 hides or 120,000 acres. The adaptation of a rural system to an urban purpose was typical of the thinking of the age in which the two were not yet separate; but if most burgesses paid dues on their land, some of them were taxed per person rather than on their holdings.

In addition to general dues, the burgesses were subject to other financial demands that reflected the status of the town, some to swell the king's coffers, some for the hierarchy of the town itself. Burgesses holding land or houses directly from the king – the majority – had to pay collectively 2 marks of silver a year. There was a supertax over and above what was normally owed to the king to pay for the supplies of the royal army when it set off on an expedition 'either on land or on sea': every household that could afford it paid 6d. In 1066 this amounted to £15.5s.3d (including £4 from the moneyers), and in fact the burgesses had to pay up whether the army was fighting that year or not, rather in the same way that income tax was imposed centuries later in time or war, only to be continued in time of peace. Another form of defence tax was the £3 that the burgesses as a group received in revenue from a strip of land held in common adjacent to the town walls; if it was needed for military purposes it went to the king, if not it went to the burgesses themselves. Down the road the obligations of the Maldon burgesses were in kind rather than money – they had to provide a horse and build a ship, confirmation of the strategic importance of the area. These were payments to the king; to the Sheriff of the town was paid £5 in gifts from the burgesses each year, with an additional 10s 8d to feed the prebendaries, presumably the community of clergy at St Botolph's. Many of these extra payments were old customs, and no doubt the burgesses were used to them, but they seem to have been less than happy about the payment which they had to make for the town mint, and which they shared with Maldon. An early Norman administrator of Colchester, Waleran, had set the figure at £20, but, as they reminded the Domesday assessors, the king 'pardoned them £10'. But far from paying the £10 they thought they should, the revenues from the mint had been granted to Walkelin, Bishop of Winchester, by 1086, and he was demanding £40 from them. The Domesday Book could record such unresolved complaints; it could also, with a note of resignation, list tax-avoiders, such as Tesco, who held two houses and 20 acres of land and owed 'customary dues to the King and never pays' or Ralph Pinel who 'has not paid the customary due and has given in a pledge' on his four houses below the town walls.

*   *   *

Such, then, was the basis of Colchester when the Anglo-Saxon rulers gave way to the Normans: a busy place, with a fertile hinterland and commerce plying up and down the river to the sea, a military centre surrounded by substantial walls, a populous town with houses beyond the confines of the walls, a number of churches, an embryonic order of canons, even a courtyard surrounded by buildings. Today, what little remains of this period must be ferreted out from the often hideous and unsympathetic contributions of modern architectural ravagers. The first thing that a visitor is now likely to see is not the Roman walls but a monstrosity of a pseudo-classical car-park in domineering brick opposite the Balkerne Gate. The destruction is not entirely modern: one Victorian publican tore down the masonry of the Balkerne Gate so that his clientele could have a better view from his pub of the new wonder of the age – steam trains arriving at the station.

Of the Norman courtyard and many of the churches, nothing is now to be found, but the Roman walls still glow, at their best opposite that spiritless car-park. St Helen's chapel also survives, if considerably altered: it still incorporates a fragment of the Roman amphitheatre and is now a museum store. But the most substantial Saxon remain is also the prettiest; the tower of Holy Trinity church. It sits at the head of a quiet little street, narrow in perspective, still clutching on to its old buildings, and, with the small shop-fronts of the adjacent Eld Street, is most redolent of the medieval street plan. Somehow the little complex avoids the shopping-centre that, monolithic, looms beside it like some great Leviathan about to swallow the last of the sprats.

Holy Trinity has its own surprises. It is surrounded by a calm graveyard, purloined by shoppers for more contemplative moments. At the doors hangs the improbable sign 'No balloons in the museum please, they can be left with the attendant', and you enter into a large interior space unexpectedly full of farm implements and exhibition cases of rural crafts – for it is no longer a church, but the Museum of Social Life[7]. Somewhere under the ploughshares and the corn dollies lies the great madrigalist, John Wilbye, as does Elizabeth I's physician, Dr William Gilbert.

Much of the church dates from the 14th century onwards, although some of the west wall of the nave pre-dates even the tower, which was built at the very beginning of the 11th century. The tower itself is tall and thin, topped by a small pyramidal roof, and looks rather like a prim and proper spinster compared to the buxom vigorousness of later medieval churches. It is instantly recognisable as Saxon by that particular geometry observed at Deerhurst, especially the doorway leading into the street, its triangular top bearing the distinctive shape of a sorcerer's hat. Its charm is partly created by the typical colours of the building materials of Colchester, the gaunt irregularities of flint being offset by the blush of reddish Roman brick, dug up from

7. Apparently small boys are in the habit of bringing in helium-filled balloons which, if accidently released, soar up into the roof and are very difficult to retrieve!

the rubble of the Roman town and here used on the corners and string courses. The effect is complimented by demure arcading high up on the tower, an idea taken to greater lengths by St Botolph's Priory, a shadow of whose west end still stands. The Priory was of a later date, and seems to have been built slowly during the 12th century. It must have been a gleam in the mind's eye of its first prior, Ainulf, at the

The Anglo-Saxon tower of Holy Trinity church, showing the extensive use of Roman brick.

time of Domesday, and in feel it is not too far removed from the Saxon aesthetic. Particularly pleasing is the double row of interlocking arches above the semi-circular west door, again executed in Roman brick. But this natural development of the decoration of the Holy Trinity tower is in itself a deception: the Normans, as if embarrassed by their lack of building materials and their trench-digging into the Roman levels, faced the whole thing with plaster into which they cut the lines of squared stonework, to create the illusion that they had imported expensive ashlar after all.

All of Colchester seems to need a more recent *doppelganger* of a building to lie unsympathetically beside the attractive old, and St Botolph's is no exception. Right beside the Norman ruins stands a Victorian church, commendable in its attempt at a neo-Norman style. But the proportions are so entirely Victorian, and the brownish-grey colour so ugly, that the execution is an unfortunate masquerade, as if the spirit of the Norman style had been subjected to the distorting mirror of an amusement arcade.

Such antiquities form a threadbare patchwork in modern Colchester, but all of them stand as a kind of preamble to the real purpose of Norman Colchester, and to the dominating architectural heritage of the town. The flourishing centre, already well fortified, exactly suited William the Conqueror's requirements for a stronghold against internal revolt and a base to guard the approaches to the Thames. Therefore around 1074 work started on that Norman symbol of dominance, a castle.

The site chosen was, as in so many other Norman sites, in a corner of the town so that the existing defences themselves became a sort of giant outer bailey wall. In Colchester the area was to the northeast corner of the town, but there is little evidence that any Saxon housing had to be cleared away to make room for the new structure, as at Wareham and elsewhere. On the contrary, the Saxon church built just near the site was retained even though it was immediately adjacent to the walls of the castle keep, and therefore a potential refuge for any attacker. It must have been a place of great holy significance, although unfortunately its import has now been long forgotten. A great ditch was dug around the site to form a moat and defend the bailey, and the earth thrown up on old Roman courtyard walls between the castle site and the Roman town-walls to create a formidable defence. The resulting bank, now bisecting a pleasant park complete with bandstand and beds of roses, is so tall and steep even today that the municipal gardener lowers his lawnmower down its slopes on the end of a long rope. The southern extremity of the bailey ditch also faintly survives in the form of a kink in the east end of the High Street that once followed its course.

Roughly in the centre of the area enclosed by the ditch the Normans could use what seemed a perfect foundation for the keep, so avoiding the problems of finding a large amount of building material and, at the same time keeping the costs down. There, probably with a heap of ruin, rubble, and stone covering it, was the base of the Roman temple of Claudius. The building material could be cleared and reused for the castle, and the foundation formed the core over which the keep would be built. In fact, the foundations were slightly too small. William built royal castles from Warwick to Pevensey, from York to Chichester, but nothing on the scale envisaged for this strategic point. Even the keep of the Tower of London (designed by Gundulph, Bishop of London, and probably the architect of Colchester Castle) is smaller in size. The Normans neatly solved the problem by using the base as the central floor of the keep, and straddled it with wall foundations 25 feet deep and 17 feet thick, narrowing a little where they emerged above ground. The giant rectangle formed is 151 feet by 110 feet, and at each corner was placed a projecting tower, rectangular except for the southeast corner, where a horseshoe shape was thrown out to contain, among other things, a chapel.

The lowest levels of the walls were easily completed using materials from the Roman remains in regular courses, bonded with Roman bricks; the first floor must have been quickly in place. Then something happened to cause the builders to stop sending the walls skyward, and hastily prepare what they had built for action. Battlements were hurriedly built around the top as if the garrison was expecting an imminent attack, and this episode almost certainly marks the invasion preparations of the Danish king, Cnut. It may be that some of the huge army that William brought over from Normandy were sent here, and the castle seemed about to fulfil the very role it was designed for, albeit before it was ready.

As soon as the alarm was over, building work continued on top of the battlements, parts of which can now be seen imbedded into the fabric. At this stage, the builders faced another problem: the ready supply of Roman building material was drying up, and the Normans had to dig deeper and deeper into the Roman remains to scavange any material at all. As a result, corner stones were brought in from the Isle of Wight, and the faces of the walls took on a less regular appearance as inferior material was utilised, some of which came from the underground central heating system of a Roman villa.

Eventually the keep towered to three stories (the walls some 80 feet high, and the corner towers 90 to 95 feet high), and dominated the town and the surrounding countryside. Inside, two huge walls ran north to south, built on to the foundations of the temple, and important to the structural integrity of the building. The entrance door in the south wall was on the level of the first floor, reached by a set of wooden steps, and incorporating a sharp internal turn to make it easier to defend. The ground floor itself was used entirely for storage, and a well was sunk whose shaft may have continued up to the first floor level, making life slightly more convenient in times of peace, and useful if the ground floor should be captured in times of war. The large hall, the focal point of the castle where communal meals were taken and administrative business conducted, seems to have occupied the west side of the keep on the first floor, stretching up two stories to the pitched roof. Elsewhere on the first floor would have been accommodation for the garrison and the kitchens, as well as the chapel in the southwest tower. The private rooms for the senior staff were probably on the second floor, and there were simple but efficient latrines in the northwest tower.

There would also have been domestic areas for the Constable of the castle, acting as administrator for the king, (one of the first was Eudo the Steward, the founder of the abbey and the leper colony). But in spite of the tapestries that adorned the walls of the hall, the rushes that covered the tiled floors, and the fires roaring away in cavernous fireplaces, Norman castles were cold and draughty places. As the keep was built, so was a large hall to the southeast, about 50 feet long and 20 feet wide. The garrison would, of course, have remained in the castle, cursing at the discomfort on a cold and blustery night, and they had the time, or the boredom, to carve little figures on the walls – Norman pictorial graffiti. But the Constable and his family almost certain resided in the relative comfort of this separate building, easier to heat but close enough to the keep to allow quick communication between the two.

*   *   *

Neither building is mentioned in the Domesday Book, as such castles were outside the aegis of the survey. Yet, not long after it was built, Colchester Castle was becoming partly redundant. The threat of a North Sea invasion was waning, and with it one of the functions of the castle. As a powerbase Colchester was too close to London for baronial ambition, which thus developed elsewhere. Equally important, the actual design of the castle was quickly out of date. Military engineers realised that if they tunnelled under one of the corner towers of a rectangular keep the tower would fall down, and, because of the structure of the building, the rest of the keep would follow suit, like a set of domino tiles. Castle-builders rapidly found the answer, experimenting first with polygonal keeps[8], and then settling for round ones – in either case, if undermined, the rest of the structure stayed intact. In those situations where a rectangular keep had already been built, an elaborate web of outer defences sprang out of the keep to defend it, best seen at Dover or the Tower of London. Colchester did develop such refinements, but nothing on the same scale. The original entrance door was replaced by a grander affair protected by its own small projecting walls with a pair of supplementary towers and the bailey curtain

8. Kilpeck castle may have had a small polygonal keep.

walls were strengthened and provided with towers and fortified gates on the west and southwest corner. These were straightforward and essential additions; that nothing more complicated was involved is a testament to the declining importance of the fortress.

There was another structural threat to the keep of which the Normans were blissfully unaware. They had fondly imagined that they had built the castle on the

The southeast wall of Colchester Castle, detailing the various stages of building materials, including a layer of Roman tiles.

147

solid Roman masonry foundations that appealed to their sense of expediency and economy. In fact, they had built it partly on sand, for the Romans, equally concerned about the costs of importing large amounts of foundation material, had designed a neat solution. Under the temple of Claudius were two long arched vaults, so that the foundations themselves were hollow. The space created was then filled with sand and sealed, unbeknown to the Normans, for their well-shaft was quite naturally sunk on the very edge of the area, and struck stone rather than sand. The resulting structure was well capable of supporting a temple, but it was never designed to cope with the stresses imposed by a Norman castle; it is a tribute to the Roman engineers that it succeeded so well. The sand was discovered by a 17th-century contractor who was attempting to demolish the building to reuse the building materials yet again. By the time he had started to clear the sand, hoping to find treasure to ease his financial problems, the top storey had been removed and one of the internal walls had collapsed. Fortunately the contractor went bankrupt before his scheme could be completed. For later generations his discovery came in useful, for the vaults, cleared of sand, served first as an ice-house, and eventually, as an air raid shelter during the Second World War.

Today, Colchester Castle is still a beautiful and satisfying building, even if it has lost its topmost storey and its bailey walls. Its sandy colours, tinged with orange and touched with the brushstroke of Roman brick-red, its firm rectangular feel and the tactile rough hue of its masonry, seem to belong to a desert or an arid landscape, the Eastern Mediterranean or an Arabian wadi. Indeed, its design is very similar to the 8th-century castle of Seyhun, suggesting a possible influence on Norman design.

Whatever its exotic associations, the local imprint is unmistakable. The long line of herringbone work in the north wall, standing out as if a weaver had changed the colour of the years, is a reminder that the masons were Saxon, even if their masters were Norman. The centre of the keep is, of course, gutted, but the large fireplaces built into the walls remain. Their openings are arch-shaped, and instead of running into chimneys the flues fan out into double exits in the sides of the walls, creating an unexpected junction of curves. From outside the castle, when the fires were lit and belching smoke, it must have looked as if there was a dragon inside snorting out smoke from his nostrils. Equally satisfying is the spacious curve of the great stone staircase that replaced the original access to the upper floors, and the large lights of the upper windows, high enough above attack to allow a wider opening, and considerably rebuilt in later years.

The tower roofs – sympathetic additions, including a cupola that reinforces the hint of the Middle East – were the work of the 18th century, and are in marked contrast to the airport-style concrete interior. The centre of the keep is now a museum, containing rather an unlikely assemblage of artifacts dominated by the carcass of the front of a 16th-century hall. Quite understandably, pride of place is given to the Roman remains, and to an extensive collection of Iron Age finds. But here and there are other treasures from different ages – illuminated books, silver plate, a model of the Civil War seige. It is one of those museums that visitors wander around with a rather bewildered air, for it is content to display rather than explain or set in context, although a model of the castle admirably shows what it might have looked like shortly after it was built. The main function of the castle from the 14th century onwards was as the major prison for the county of Essex and, as a result, this section of the castle has survived largely intact.

If you wander past the long rows of glass cases holding Roman urns, find your way through the maze of the upper floor into what was once the open space of the chapel, and hunt around a little, you will at last find something that is Saxon. There stands a cabinet of weapons containing a huge swinging battle-axe, a thrusting spear, a shield of hide with a proud boss of the very type that littered the shore after the battle of Maldon. No hand holds them and they grace no arm; they are dominated by a life-sized figure nearby. It is the model of a Norman soldier, commanding the centre of the floor in chain-mail and conical helmet. The juxtaposition seems to epitomise Colchester: a true city of Britain, an ancient kingdom's capital, a Roman fortress, an Anglo-Saxon town, a Norman stronghold. Three of those periods we revere; we visit their remains, we teach their history, we are excited at every new discovery. The fourth – the Anglo-Saxon – we are inclined to ignore, to relegate to a small cabinet in the corner of an alien chapel.

That Norman soldier knew better. It seems appropriate, having started with the Welsh looking down from their mountains to the thrusting new *mottes* of the continental invaders, to end with a Norman standing on the battlements of one of the great symbols of conquest, Colchester Castle, gazing across to the open sea, waiting for another invasion that never came. He knew that, without the legacy of the Anglo-Saxons – the towns and the villages, the farming systems, the sophisticated administration, the laws, the scholarly learnings, the very nature of the people themselves – the Norman achievement would not have been possible. We know that it was that very synthesis – the fusion of Norman discipline and drive and Anglo-Saxon adaptability and inventiveness – that shifted the axis of the development of the country. This synthesis ensured that England would never again be split up into petty kingdoms, and determined that, however many anxious moments were spent gazing across the seas in later years, the country would never again be conquered by alien force-of-arms. From that unity, from those Anglo-Saxon traditions and those Norman ideas, the rest of our history has sprung.

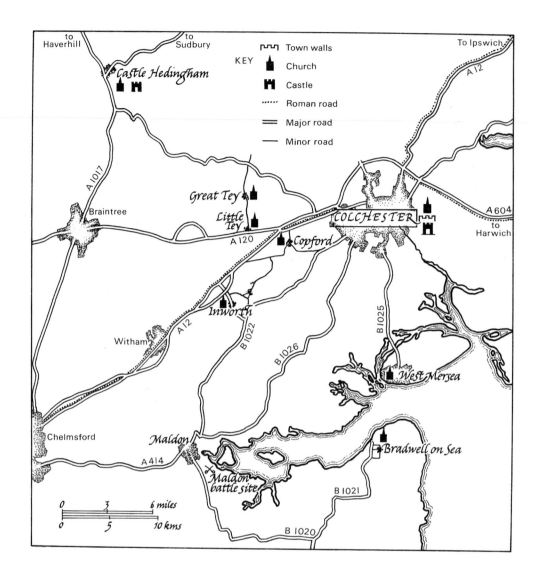

150

Traveller's Guide

Location of Colchester

From Chelmsford (22 miles) and London (53 miles), A12 east. From Ipswich (18 miles), A12 west. Train services from London and Ipswich.

Castle TL 999254: (metric map 168; 1-inch map 162). The castle is in the centre of the modern town at the east end of the High Street.

Holy Trinity Church TL 996252: The church is a few minutes' walk from the southwest of the castle in Trinity Street.

St Botolph's Priory TL 999249: The priory ruins are south of the castle, down Queen Street.

Tourist Information Office: situated in the Town Hall on the north side of the High Street. Publications include a comprehensive Guide to the town.

Parking: there are a number of car-parks on the south of the centre of the town, just outside the Roman walls, and the large one to the west in Balkerne Street, which is particularly convenient. It should be noted that there are no road signs to the castle so visitors should follow the signs to the town centre.

Maldon From Colchester (16 miles) B1022. From Chelmsford (10 miles) and London (41 miles) A414 southeast of Chelmsford.

Maldon Battle site TL 866054: take B1018 south of Maldon. $\frac{1}{2}$ mile south of the town there is a row of isolated houses to the left-hand side of the road, and in the middle a lane leading through a farm to the site.

Other local Anglo-Saxon and Norman sites

Bradwell-on-Sea TM 031082: The Church of St Cedd: Famous early Saxon church (7th century); the nave survives as an isolated building.

Castle Hedingham TL 787358: Castle: spectacular keep (1141) in excellent state of preservation. Church: large 12th-century church with carvings.

Copford TL 935277: Church of St Michael and All Angels: 12th-century church with famous and heavily restored wall-paintings.

Inworth TL 879178: Inworth church: Late Anglo-Saxon nave and chancel.

Great Tey TL 891258: Large and beautiful church. Lower half of tower may be late Anglo-Saxon (though not mentioned in guide to church); the upper half, with attractive round-headed windows and recesses and use of brick, is Norman.

Little Tey TL 893237: Norman church close to above.

West Mersea TM 008125: 11th-century tower in church which was founded in 8th or 9th century.

Similar sites elsewhere in England

Colchester Castle is an unusual survival, and there are no obvious parallels other than the mass of 12th-century castles spread around the country. The other major royal castles are to be found at the Tower of London (whose White Tower (the keep) has obvious similarities to Colchester), Dover and Windsor.

Other major castle ruins where building work from the time of William I survives include:

Chepstow, Gwent ST 533941 (metric map 162; 1-inch map 155): The earliest stone castle in Britain (started before 1071), now a massive and imposing site.

Corfe, Dorset. Details listed in the chapter on Wareham.

Exeter, Devon SX 918933 (metric map 192; 1-inch map 176): remains of 1068 gatehouse.

Richmond, Yorkshire NZ 174006 (metric map 92; 1-inch map 91): substantial remains of early Norman castle begun in the 1070s.

BIBLIOGRAPHY

The following bibliography is confined to those books and publications that might be of interest to the general reader. For readers who wish to study the period in greater depth or detail, most of the books below have comprehensive bibliographies that include the more academic studies. The titles in italic lettering are available in paperback.

GUIDES AND RELATED PUBLICATIONS

General: *A Guide to Anglo-Saxon Sites*, Nigel and Mary Kerr, Granada Paladin 1983: a comprehensive guide to major and minor sites with short entries for each site. *A Guide to Norman Sites in Britain*, Nigel and Mary Kerr, Granada Paladin 1984: a companion to the above. *Anglo-Saxon and Norman* in the Buildings of Britain series, Alastair Service, Barrie & Jenkins 1982: less detailed than the Paladin guides, but with a more comprehensive gazetteer.

Kilpeck: *Guide* to church and *Reproduction of Victorian drawings* of the carvings available in the church.

Deerhurst: *Guide* to church and other related publications available in the church.

Wareham: *Guide and history* of town; *leaflet* in the Making of Dorset series available in the Tourist Information Centre. *Guides* to the churches available in the churches and in the Tourist Information Centre. *Poole Bay and Purbeck 300 BC–AD 1660*, C. Cochrane, The Friary Press 1970: this gives an interesting historical survey of the area.

Savernake Forest and Great Bedwyn: *A History of Savernake Forest*, The Marquess of Ailesbury. Private printing 1962. This interesting book may still be found in Marlborough bookshops, and is held in Marlborough library.

Newton Bromswold: There is no specific guide to the village remains. *Rushden: A Duchy of Lancaster Village*, David Hall and Ruth Harding, Buscott 1985: this mainly covers nearby Rushden, but includes information on Newton Bromswold and the immediate area. Although this is the product of much research and very detailed, it is a model of its kind and of interest to the general reader and the academic alike.

St Fagan's Folk Museum: Guide to Hendre'r-Ywdd Uchaf available in museum bookshop.

Greensted: *Guide* to church available in church.

Brixworth: *Guide* to church and related publications available in the church.

Colchester: *Guide* to Colchester, *Guide* to Colchester town, and survey *In Search of Colchester's Past* (including a short bibliography) available at the Tourist Information Centre in the Town Hall and in the bookshop in the castle Museum.

THE DOMESDAY BOOK

Facsimile Edition: The complete Domesday Book, with a facsimile of the original opposite a translation, and with comprehensive notes, maps, and introductions, has been published by

Phillimore in the series History from the Sources, general editor John Morris. Each county is given a separate volume (or volumes), available in both paperback and hardback. In the same series are many issues of related material.

Guide: *Domesday Book: A Guide*, R. Welldon Finn, Phillimore 1973.

Children's Guide: The Children's Book of Domesday England, Peter Boyden, illustrated by David Salariya and Shirley Willis. Kingfisher, in association with the English Tourist Board 1985.

Maps: Ordnance Survey publish two useful titles, each with two maps (1:625,000 or about 10 miles to the inch) covering north and south Britain, in book form with accompanying texts and very comprehensive gazetteers and bibliographies: Britain Before the Norman Conquest and Monastic Britain.

HISTORIES

General: The two major surveys of the period are in the Oxford History of England: Vol II: Anglo-Saxon England, Sir Frank Stenton and Vol III: From Domesday Book to Magna Carta, A.L. Poole.

Major Paperback series: The Pelican History of England: *The Beginnings of English Society*, Dorothy Whitelock. *English Society in the Early Middle Ages*, Doris Stenton, Penguin: both are authoritative and readable introductions to the period, although occasionally overtaken by more recent research and discoveries.
The Making of Britain: *The Norman Heritage 1066–1200*, Trevor Rowley, Granada Paladin: less interesting than the Penguin series, but very well illustrated.
The Fontana History of England (*Rural England 1066–1272* H.E. Hallam) and The Pelican Economic History of Britain (*Medieval Economy and Society* M.M. Postan) are more for the specialist than the general reader.

Anglo-Saxons and Normans: Of the many books available, *Anglo-Saxon England and the Norman Conquest*, H.R. Loyn, Longman 1962 and *The Norman Conquest*, H.R. Loyn, Hutchinson 1965, are notable. Perhaps the most readable book on the period is The Normans and their World, Jack Lindsay, Hart-Davis MacGibbon, 1973. This explores the European background and the activities of Normans elsewhere as well as late Anglo-Saxon and Norman England.

Place names: The standard work is The Concise Oxford Dictionary of English Place Names, Eilert Ekwall. Oxford 4th edition 1960.

RECORDS

Easter Mass: Anglo-Saxon Easter, The Schola Gregoriana of Cambridge, Archiv 413 546–1, 1984. Recording of the reconstructed Winchester texts made in Deerhurst church.

INDEX